The Relic:

Jerusalem to St. Augustine, Fl.

A HISTORICAL, INSPIRATIONAL, ECUMENICAL-TIME TRAVEL, MYSTERY THAT CONFIRMS THE EXISTENCE OF GOD.

K. Ross Lee
And
Betsy S. Lee

Copyright ©2018 by K. Ross Lee and Betsy S. Lee

All rights are reserved. No part of this book shall be reproduced or transmitted in any form or by any means, electronic, mechanical, photographic including photocopying, recording, or by any information storage and retrieval system, without prior written permission of the publishers. No patent liability is assumed with respect to the use of the information contained herein. Although every precaution has been taken in the preparation of this book, the publisher and authors assume no responsibility for errors or omissions. Neither is any liability assumed for damage resulting from the use of the information contained herein.

Creating Worlds from Words

This is a work of fiction. Names, characters, places, and incidents either are the product of the author's imagination or are used fictitiously. Any resemblance to persons, living or dead is entirely coincidental.

ISBN-978-0-692-10887-1

Published by: Kalmun R. Lee and Betsy S. Lee 2018

Cover design and photos by Betsy S. Lee

Info@betsyslee.com

Printed in the United States of America, Elkton, Florida 32033

Forward

Authors comment:

The following explains that time can, at least in theory, be changed.

Einstein's Theory of General relativity provides our modern understanding of space, time and gravity -- which means it's crucial to almost everything we do in physics and astronomy. The reason everyone should know about relativity pertains to the way it changes our perception of reality. Relativity tells us that our ordinary perceptions of time and space are not universally valid. Instead, space and time are intertwined as four-dimensional space-time.

In our ordinary lives, we perceive only three dimensions—length, width and depth—and we assume that this perception reflects reality. However, in space-time context, time must be added to the equation, along with length, width, and depth.[1]

---

[1] Why They Matter" (Columbia University Press, 2014). Jeffrey Bennett, author of "What is Relativity?

In memory of

Mae Arenofsky

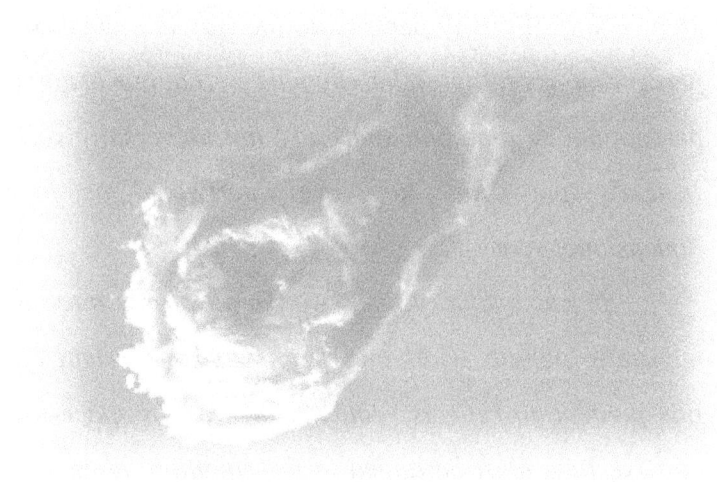

"We are a formless blob when we enter this world, unaware of our surroundings or ourselves. Molded by circumstances, we are continuously changing."
                                                             Betsy S. Lee

ACKNOWLEDGMENTS

In no particular order, a special thanks to all our friends who gave tirelessly of their time and patience.
Aileen Q. Wietstruk, Nancy Quatrano *(On-Target Words: Professional Writing Services)*, Kareen Saum, Jackie Hashagen, Bob & Ruth Feldheim, Abe Cohen, the Ladies from *Broader Horizons Book Club,* Dr. Dorothy Headley Israel, Jennifer Roche.

Part I

"Behold, I stand at the door and knock: If any man hears my voice, and open the door, I will come to him.

Revelation 3:20

The Relic: Jerusalem to St. Augustine

*"Even though I walk through the valley of the shadow of death,
I will fear no evil, for You are with me;
With rod and staff, You comfort me...."*

Psalm 23

Will Papa Die?

The bugs, the birds, Carol lying on a pile of leaves, her bloody hands covering her face ...

The horror of it faded as I abruptly awoke to my cell phone's buzz and vibration. The small alarm clock on the night table displayed 3 a.m. *Who the hell is calling me at this hour?*

It was my father's old friend, and partner, Professor Arenofsky. "It's your father. He's at Flagler Hospital.

He's suffered a heart attack."

My gut tightened, I almost choked on the words, "Is he dead?"

"Joel, you're just like him–always jumping to conclusions. He's alive. In ICU."

"Oh, my God! What happened?

"We had a late dinner and planned to return to the office for our quarterly business meeting.

During dinner, he suddenly stood up, his face ashen, grabbed his left arm, and grimaced in pain.

"He needed to be rushed to the hospital. He refused, insisted he'd be fine. Hashem was going to help him. You know how stubborn he can be." My nightmare came back, Papa's voice reverberating in my head, *She'll be all right. Hashem will look after her.*

Professor Arenofsky went on, "He cried in pain. I pleaded with him to let me call an ambulance. He agreed, provided I'd take him to Flagler Hospital."

Fear and shame swept over me at his words, his voice replaced by a faint buzzing of that memory. *Mama in the ambulance—the scream of the siren. Papa and I following close behind. My repeating, "I should have walked with her."*

All the way to the hospital, he kept repeating, 'I must pass on the Kabbalah's secret to Joel. He's the last male descendant of the House of David.'

As we pulled into the emergency entrance, he gasped for air, saying something about finding Aaron's breastplate. Do you have any idea what that's all about?"

"Not a clue."

"You and Carol must leave for the hospital, now. There's not a moment to lose."

"Yes. We'll leave right away."

"Let me know when you arrive. I'm at the Casa Monica Hotel.

In a state of shock, I rushed to Carol's bedroom, paused in the doorway, and stared into the blackness. *Is death like this, a dark nothingness?* Papa wouldn't see it that way. His philosophy was; *As long as the soul lives in the body, it is limited to the body's physical perceptions.* But when the body dies, the soul is released to higher spiritual realities. Soul? Did I even believe one exists? I turned the lights on. Carol lay in a fetal position wrapped in a thin, red-plaid quilt. "Carol wake up, wake up."

I shook her shoulder, but she brushed my hand aside, and grumbled, "Go away."

"Carol, Papa's had a heart attack. He's in the ICU."

She popped-up from under the quilt and blinked like a startled owl. I watched the color drain out of her face.

"Professor Arenofsky just called. We must leave now."

"Is he going to die?" she whispered.

Die? He always seemed invincible. "How the hell should I know? Just hurry up."

Her face flushed with terror. "Do you think he'll understand our situation?"

"I don't know."

"What if he doesn't?"

"You're just like Mama, worrying about things which haven't happened, yet. Hurry, get dressed, it's a long drive from Princeton to St. Augustine."

Carol

The streetlights eked out dim rays through the mist. We rushed to my beat-up old Toyota without saying a word. Carol entered on the passenger side, I opened the hatchback and threw our bags in, and then I plopped into the driver's seat.

Carol was on her cell phone. "There's a family emergency. I won't be in. Please cover for me. I'll call you as soon as I know something."

She dropped her phone into her pocketbook. "Let's go." At that pre-dawn hour, the drive on I-95 south was monotonous. The sight of huge oak trees took me back in time to when we were children living in Spring Valley, New York.

Colorful annuals, copious azalea bushes, and massive lush purplish- pink rhododendrons lined the curved, stone-paved driveway.

Papa, an Orthodox Jewish scholar, is authoritarian. He always dressed in a white shirt, a rumpled dark-blue suit and a vest with fringes called Tzitzit that peeked out from under his jacket. A small black yamaka sat precariously on his shiny, bald head. A long, gray, shaggy beard covered part of his eggplant-shaped body. When in contemplation or upset, he habitually stroked his beard, especially when Carol or I broke one of the archaic 613 Laws of Moses, as though it was one of the Ten Commandments.

Each evening, Mama and Papa would retire to our library off the foyer, and sit on over-stuffed, green velveteen armchairs. Mama's hand-crocheted doilies adorned the chairs' arms and backs.

The library ritual never changed. They discussed the day's events. Papa read. Mama read.

The nightly ritual before going to bed too was etched in stone. Papa would kiss us on the forehead, and say, "Good nicht, my kinder."

Mama too kissed us on the forehead. "Pleasant dreams."

On occasion, Carol and I would sit on the top landing, listening to their conversations. At times, their private talk would be in Yiddish, and we didn't completely understand them.

The night before Carol was to go to her friend's birthday party, and I to my baseball practice, we heard them arguing about Carol's new party dress.

Papa's voice blared. "She's not going to wear the new dress. It's too short. I know how boys think!"

Carol cupped her face and sobbed. "Joel, the dress he wants me to wear is old-fashioned and too long."

"You're crying over the length of your dress?" I whispered, amazed that such a thing could be of any importance.

"Yes, my friends are going to make fun of me."

Mama almost never contradicted Papa, but that night she did. "Papa, you make such harsh judgments. It's the twentieth century. Carol has to be fashionable."

Papa bellowed, "You mean the way she dresses will make her acceptable?"

"Keep your voice down, you'll wake the kinder. Papa, your imagination carries you away. She'll be all right."

We strained to hear Papa's low-pitched voice, "Okay, okay; it's going against my better judgment—let her wear it! But Joel must walk her to and from the party."

I made a face; Carol poked me in the side.

Papa's voice trailed off. All we heard finally was, "Thank you, dear. You're doing a mitzvah. Carol will be so happy."

Carol smiled, kissed my cheek, and off to bed we went.

The Relic: Jerusalem to St. Augustine

The next morning, Mama and Carol's voices drifted up to my bedroom, "Carol don't forget to take the gift."

Carol whined, "Ma ..."

Mama called up to me, "Joel hurry up. You have to walk your sister to the birthday party."

Must I? "I'm getting dressed, Ma." She stepped on my words.

"Your aunt Sarah is coming over in a few minutes to help me with the Passover Seder. Hurry up, or Carol will be late."

Carols' whining drifted up, "Ma, I don't need Joel or anybody to walk me. I'm almost nine years old."

My heart lightened. She doesn't need me. *Thank God.*

Kvetching, Carol continued. "Ma, please, it's not far. I'm in fourth grade."

"My kinder, Papa would be very angry if I let you go by yourself." A few moments of silence followed. Mama's voice lightened, "However, you are growing up fast."

I could picture Mama standing with arms folded as Carol pleaded.

"But I'll be late for the party. Please, please, Mama, please, I got all A's on my report card and—"

"I'm going against my better judgment, Carol. Promise not to tell Papa," I heard Carol say as I buckled my pants and looked around my room.

"I promise. I promise," Carol nearly squealed. She sounded like she was dancing.

I stopped to listen. Mama hesitated. "Now go directly to the party and call when you get there."

"I will." Carol's voice sounded happy.

"Joel, what in the world is taking so long?"

Mama shouted to me.

I looked around on the floor in my room and frowned. "Can't find my catcher's mitt."

"It's on the top shelf in your closet."

Mama *knows everything*. I grabbed it, ran down the stairs, and stopped in the kitchen. She stood over the hot stove, perspiring as she stirred a big wooden spoon in a pot, her words in cadence with each stir. "Please try to catch up to Carol. Run, if you half to. She's gotten a good start on you." *I'm never going to be a cook.* "Yeah, I'm outta here ..." I yelled over my shoulder and headed for the door.

How great it's going to be that my sister will not have to rely on me so much.

I'm not sure why, but I noticed there were no chirping birds from the familiar wooded lot that I passed on my way to baseball practice.

Instead, giant black birds screeched wildly and flapped their wings as though their lives depended on it. I got a shiver and gripped my mitt tighter. The sound of moaning came from behind some bushes. Curious, I ventured in.

Scared of what I'd find, my mind repeated what Papa taught me. *"You are a mensch when you always do the right things for others and yourself no matter what happens."* In spite of my fears, I had to see what was making the awful moaning.

Tucking my mitt into the waist of my pants, I took a deep breath and ventured in further.

Big, black, evil birds with vulture-like talons and beaks, stared with beady eyes from above. It was unnerving, glancing side-to-side; I avoided branches, while I swatted bugs off my arms and face. The moaning grew louder. My heart pounded.
It was Carol—in the dirt, holding her head, blood ran between her fingers. Blood-soaked leaves and twigs tangled in her golden blond hair—the new party dress, dirty and torn.

The blackbirds were ready to swoop down on us. "Go away, get out of here!" I shouted. I threw stones at the squawking birds. They screamed as they flew off in a flurry.

Trembling, I bent down and put my arm behind Carol to help her sit up. Pulling her bloody hands away from her face, I saw a deep gash across her forehead.

My stomach turned when I saw the bone of her left pinkie finger sticking out, the fingertip hanging by a thread of skin.

The Relic: Jerusalem to St. Augustine

She paled and screamed, "My finger!"

I held her tight, "You'll be OK."

She began to shiver and shook her head as she looked at me with tear-filled eyes. "There were three of them, I—I—was walking—," she pointed in the direction of the sidewalk.

"Suddenly, three boys stopped me." Bloody tears ran down her cheeks. "They wanted the present. I wouldn't let go. One of them hit me—another pushed me—I fell—screaming and kicking. They dragged me here. Two of them held me down and forced the gift out of my hands. The other one tried to lay on top of me—I spit in his face. He jumped up, saying terrible things. Then they ran away laughing." Carol held her head, moaned, and slumped in my arms.

The Portrait

A blast of a car horn brought me back to the present. We passed a highway sign near Richmond: VCU, School of Medicine. My mind flashed back to the day I received a strange letter from Carol.

My Dearest Brother,

I hope this letter finds you well. You often told me to be more social. Ever since middle school, I knew my so-called friends made fun of my deformity behind my back.

If you thought my high school experience was bad, medical school is much worse. I met with my school's psychologist; he recommended I meet with him on a regular basis. However, I know I can handle it without his help. I'm strong and can make the necessary lifestyle changes.

I have left medical school and have taken a position as a pharmaceutical representative. Please don't worry, the job pays well, and I will be able to work a territory alone.

Your Loving Sister,
Carol

ואו

My thoughts were interrupted when Carol said, "Joel, I have to pee."

Just like a woman. "I'll pull off at Alexandria. Hang on, it's the next exit."

Carol had her hand on the door handle, as we parked. She swung the door open, ran out, and shouted, "Meet you in the restaurant."

The restaurant was jammed. I got on a long line. A deep voice reached my ears over the clamor.

"Joel, Joel Schwartz, over here."

I glanced in the direction of the voice. It was one of Papa's oldest friends and clients, the curator at the West Building of the National Gallery of Art in DC.

Carol rejoined me and followed the direction of my gaze. "Look over there. it's Dr. Jordan!"

We left the line and headed toward him.

He stood as we approached and extended his hand to us, his smile warm. "I haven't seen the two of you in years. Please join me."

The Relic: Jerusalem to St. Augustine

His appearance had changed from when we'd last met.

What was once a full head of brown wavy hair was now wisps of white strands. Deep lines etched his ruddy complexion.

But his waxed handlebar mustache with turned-up tips and his distinctive voice were the same.

"How's your father?" He inquired as Carol tugged at her glove. Her eyes welled up.

The waiter appeared and took our order. Carol said she wasn't hungry. I insisted she has something to eat; we still had a long ride ahead of us. The waiter left. Again, Dr. Jordan asked about Papa.

I told him what we knew. "He's in critical condition in St. Augustine. We're on our way to be with him."

"I'm very sorry to hear that. Do you two know how your father and I met?"

"No," I answered for both of us.

He smiled and nodded. "I was on the thirteenth-century art staff at the National Gallery.

The university gave him a retirement dinner, and the entire museum staff was invited. It's because of him I have my current position."

Carol responded, "I didn't know."

Dr. Jordan gave the tip of his mustache a twist. "My life transformed dramatically about a year later when your father informed me he had become a custom antiquity dealer. He said he could acquire an original piece of art from any era. I laughed at him. Your father went on a tirade. He said he would never lie to me.

I challenged him to produce Leonardo da Vinci's thirteenth-century portrait of Ginevra de' Benci, with a deadline of thirty days, knowing the provenance was lost centuries ago. He took the challenge. Less than a week later, he called and asked to see me privately. Convinced I was going to hear an apology, I arranged to have him come to my office at 2:15 the next afternoon.

Punctual as usual, he arrived carrying a sizable flat box, leaned it up against my desk and proudly announced, 'Here it is!'

He helped me take it out of the box. We tore the portrait's wrapping away, exposing the carved, ornate gold, wood frame. It was, indeed, the portrait Ginevra de' Benci.

I asked, "But is it authentic?

"Your father smiled and assured me, it was real."

Carol's face reflected my confusion.

I blurted, "Was it?"

"Yes. We ran every imaginable test and consulted with the world's most respected da Vinci experts. They authenticated the portrait."

He picked up his coffee and took a long sip. "From then on, your father fulfilled my every request. As a result, I got rapid promotions. It did not take long before he developed a client list of the world's major collectors!"

Dr. Jordan raised an eyebrow, paused, leaned in, "What a tragedy it would be to lose your father and his secret of how he acquired things. Did he ever confide in either of you?"

"The only thing he told us was, 'the secret was hidden in the Kabbalah.' I've been analyzing it for years, but I've been unable to find the key."

He took a deep breath and sighed. "I sincerely hope your father's recovering. Please give him my regards."

"Of course."

Shanda

When we crossed the state line from Virginia into North Carolina, Carol was asleep, leaning against the door. I looked at her and sighed, checked the mirrors, and adjusted my grip on the steering wheel. My thoughts wandered back to the day I received my Ph.D.

"*Mazel Tov,*" Papa said in his booming voice. He shook my hand and beamed. "*You have brought nachas to your dear departed Mama and me.*"

We drove to our apartment, to celebrate with champagne. Carol drove Papa in his car. I hoped she wouldn't say anything about us sharing a bedroom.

We parked only a few spaces away from each other. I watched as Papa opened the trunk and took out a big gift-wrapped box.

Carol walked over to me, and I whispered, "Have you told him?"

She put a finger to her lips, "Shush. No. He's coming."

It was only seconds before he was standing in front of us and asked what the two of us were up to? I asked him to let me take the box.

He said, "No, I can handle it."

Once inside the apartment, Papa asked where he could put the gift. Carol indicated the living room, on the coffee table. Then she went to get the champagne.

Papa carefully placed the gift on the table and inquired where the bathroom was.

Down the hall, I told him. Off he went.

The Relic: Jerusalem to St. Augustine

Carol returned with the champagne. I asked her how we could bring up the subject of our temporarily sharing a bedroom.

A burst of hysterics came from down the hall, "It's a **Shanda!** My children are sleeping together!"

Wide-eyed, tugging at his beard, red-faced, neck veins bulging he came into the living room, and bellowed, "You two are an abomination! My children are dead to me!" Pounding on his chest, he recited the mourner's prayer—*"Yit-ga-dal ve-yit-ka-dash she-mei ra-ba—"*

As Papa rushed out the door, Carol cried, "Don't Papa, don't! Papa, it's not what you think"!

שׁשׁשׁ

Carol's screamed, "Watch out, you're going to hit that car!" I swerved back into our lane just in time, barely missing the car to my left.

"What's wrong with you?" Carol snapped. "You're going to get us killed!"

I didn't answer.

Flagler Hospital

The setting sun threw long shadows through the stately palm trees that lined the road to the hospital entrance. The parking lot was full. Luckily, a car pulled out of a space near the emergency entrance, just as we arrived.

A half-dozen people sat in the spacious lobby. Scenic watercolor paintings hung on the walls.

A male nurse in green scrubs sat in a glass cubicle, focused on his computer screen. Speaking through a small opening in the glass, I asked, "What is the condition of Professor Schwartz?"

He looked up. "Are you relatives?"

"Yes, we're his children," I replied, fighting the panic growing in my chest.

"Spell the name please."

I did, enunciating each letter. "Is Mrs. Schwartz here?"

"She passed away long ago," I muttered.

He resumed working at his computer. We waited in silence, Carol shifting her weight from one foot to the other.

Finally, he looked up at us. "One moment, please, while I call someone who can discuss your father's condition with you."

Carol started to speak, but he interrupted and pointed to chairs in a corner. "Please have a seat. Someone will be with you in a few minutes."

The few minutes seemed like an eternity. A broad-shouldered, middle-aged woman in green scrubs and a white lab jacket, with the nameplate 'C. K. Smith RN' approached us.

"Are you Professor Benjamin Schwartz's children?"

We stood. I nodded, and the nurse sighed. "Let's sit down."

Carol reached for my hand, and I held on for dear life. The nurse shook her head.

"I'm sorry. Professor Schwartz passed away a short while ago."

Carol crushed my hand.

"He suffered a massive stroke. We did everything possible, but we couldn't save him." She cleared her throat. "He had a message for you. He said he forgave you."

My heart sank. "Were you there? What were his last words, exactly?" I growled.

"His last words were, 'I unconditionally forgive my children.'"

Carol paled and then covered her face, trembling and crying. Her voice faltered. "He's gone. We didn't make it in time. But at least, he finally forgave us."

Pulling her close, I felt her warm tears on my neck. I whispered, "He had to, Carol. He truly believed if he didn't, God wouldn't forgive him for not forgiving us.

The Relic: Jerusalem to St. Augustine

Papa would want us to celebrate his life. The Torah states that there is an existence after death.

Our soul returns to God so it can continue to serve Hashem. *'Baruch dayan eme,* blessed is the one true Judge."

Leaning back and wiping her tears, Carol said, "I know, I know. He also believed in *Oleam Ha Ba,* the world to come, a higher state of being, As far as I'm concerned, dead is dead, and that's all there is!"

שששׁ

We made our way to Papa, in silence.

I expected the morgue to be a refrigerated room with human-sized filing drawers. However, it was simply a big, quiet room with gurneys lining the walls. A few of the gurneys held bodies covered with sheets. Carol clutched her elbows, her eyes darting from left to right, around the room.

The morgue attendant asked, "May I assist you?"

"We're looking for Professor Benjamin Schwartz."

"Follow me."

He guided us to a gurney in a corner. He pulled the sheet down, exposing Papa's colorless face, and solemnly asked, "Is this Professor Schwartz?"

"Yes."

"I'll leave you alone," he said as he turned and walked away.

Carol sobbed, "I just can't believe Papa's gone. We all missed so much."

"You couldn't reason with him. We certainly tried, but he wouldn't hear us out."

Carol kissed Papa on the cheek and started to cry

I recited the Shema (the acknowledgment of the one God), "She-ma Yis-ra-eil A-do-nai E-lo-hei-nu, A-do-nei E-chad! Ba-ruch sheim ke-vod mal-chu-to le-a-lam va-ed."

Carol joined in. "Hear, O Israel: the Lord is our God, the Lord is one! Blessed is His glorious kingdom forever and ever."

We stared at Papa's lifeless body, lost in our own thoughts.

My mind jumped back in time: *I should have walked her to the party.*

Mama told me Carol had been traumatized and would need to see a mental health professional.

Papa refused to consider her therapy. He felt she was strong enough to get over it all.

I catered to Carol: served her milk and cookies, filled her glass with fresh water, and brought her anything of mine she wanted.

I even gave up watching the World Series. I became my sister's slave–and I loved it.

From that day forward, Carol hid her left hand from view, by wearing gloves or keeping her fist clenched.

The morgue attendant's tap on my shoulder jerked me back to reality. He asked if we were through.

I nodded 'yes.' Carol wiped her eyes.

But I hoped in my heart that we weren't.

I nodded 'yes.' Carol wiped her eyes.
But I hoped in my heart that we weren't.

The Sword of Islam

*P*apa's home in St. Augustine was surrounded by fragrant gardenia bushes. A stately old Victorian with two turrets and a wraparound porch, the painted lady, resided on the quiet southern end of St. George Street, the rear-facing Lake Sanchez.

Entering the old house, I pondered what Carol had said in the hospital. *"It's too bad we all missed so much."*

It wasn't true. As children, we did things together, like sailing on his catamaran as he pointed out historic places such, as Castillo de San Marcos, the Great Cross at the Mission of *Nombre de Dios*, and the Fountain of Youth.

He'd take us around the house pointing out new artifacts he'd collected from around the world.

I'll never forget the day we lingered at a new wall display: Five swords arranged in a fan shape; the center one had a gold tassel hanging from its ornate pommel, and the letters' JC etched in the blade.

Papa explained, "Those swords belonged to our ancestors," Boasting, "No one in the world can acquire the things I can. I always get the better of the El-Khattab, (Sword of Islam.)"

"Papa, how do you do that?" I'd asked.

Pushing his glasses higher on his nose, he's said, "*Pe'ulat ha-koah,* it's in the Kabbalah, and someday, my son, you will understand, after you discover the map."

I'd retorted, "Papa, you gave me an English copy of the Kabbalah. But you never gave me a map."

He'd put his arm around me, chuckled and said, "When the time is right, you'll have the map. It will lead to the greatest treasure of all time!" He laughed. "My son, maybe it's hidden in the attic–perhaps not!"

The next day I needed to learn what arrangements Papa had made for his finale parting.

I figured the first place to look was on the second floor, in his private office.

My heart pounded. I paused, turned the doorknob slowly, Papa's words echoing, '*The two of you are not to go into my study.*'

Carol's voice broke the silence. "Open the door already, Joel."

On the opposite wall were an impressive floor-to-ceiling, wall-to-wall bookcase packed-full of old, worn books, and hand-penned manuscripts, in English, Hebrew, and Greek. Against the wall to the left was a large antique oak roll-top desk, with packed cubbyholes. On the wall above the desk hung two oil paintings, one of the Masada fortress, the other of Rabbi Baal Shem Tov, founder of Hasidic Judaism.

Carol stood in front of the Masada picture and remarked, "Joel, someday I'm going to visit Israel, and stand on the ground of our Martyrs."

I laughed, "Sure! Now help me find what we came here for, and keep your eyes open for a treasure map."

After looking through all his possessions, I finally found what we were seeking, a contract for a prepaid gravesite at the King David Cemetery, in Jacksonville.

I phoned the cemetery and explained the need for an orthodox rabbi. They were pleasant and suggested calling the Etz Chaim Synagogue in Jacksonville.

While waiting for someone to pick up the phone, another flash from the past came over me: *Bubbie once said, 'If you have to choose smart, rich, or lucky, always pick lucky.'* Today I'd be lucky. Not just any Rabbi was available, but the one who had known Papa for many years.

We made the burial arrangements for Sunday, the first day after the Sabbath.

The Relic: Jerusalem to St. Augustine

In preparation for sitting Shiva, Carol covered the mirrors in the house, just as Mama had done when Bubbie died. When I was a kid, my mind had the notion the spirit from the dead wouldn't get lost on its journey back to God. However, Papa taught me differently. The mirrors are covered because to look at your reflection is considered idolatrous when one's only thoughts should be of God.

שׁשׁשׁ

Immediately after the funeral, we went back to Papa's house where we started the seven-day ritual of sitting Shiva.

There we received the condolences, platters of fruit, and food from relatives and friends.

Professor Ira Arenofsky, whose small stature deceptively concealed his huge intellect, was Papa's partner and best friend. They were roommates at Yeshiva College, in New York City. Still slim and dignified, with a neatly trimmed mustache and goatee, his pale skin defied the fact that he lived in Florida.

I took notice of the professor and a group of people standing by the dining room table, engrossed in animated conversation. Carol and I meandered over.

Standing next to my obese cousin, Susan was a tall, thin redhead.

A strong scent of perfume emanated from her décolletage, which displayed generous mounds of breasts. Under her dramatic eyebrows, coal-smudged eyelids heightened her beautiful blue eyes.

"Did Professor Schwartz live in this house all his life? Where did the antiques come from? Did anyone find a map?" she asked, in shotgun fashion, with a French accent.

Her questions unnerved me. Interrupting I asked the professor, "And who might this lovely woman be?"

"Oh, I'm sorry, Joel; I didn't see you and Carol standing there. Forgive me. This is Joel and Carol, Professor Schwartz's children; and this is Ms. Krief, an Adjunct Professor from Morocco."

She flashed a film star smile. "Nice to meet both of you."

After some small talk, we excused ourselves on the pretext we were going for some fresh air.

Once outside, Carol remarked, "I think Ms. Krief is a phony."

"Why do you say that?"

"Look at the way she's dressed!"

"What's wrong with it?"

"An Adjunct Professor couldn't afford an expensive Halston-designer dress."

"How would you know it's expensive?"

"My dear brother, I'm a charter Vogue subscriber."

By ten o'clock, everyone was gone except Cousin Susan, who was sleeping over. She was afraid to drive at night.

As Carol and I cleaned up, Susan washed the dishes. Half asleep, she said, "This is the last of the dirty dishes, thank God."

"God had nothing to do with it," I refuted. "God has everything to do with everything," she countered. "It's been a long day, and I'm going to bed." She bade us good night and left the room.

Carol suggested, "Let's look for the map now."

"Shouldn't we wait until the Shiva period is over?"

"It doesn't matter. Papa's gone."

"All right, let's do it. We'll go through the backyard and around through the old servant's entrance."

"Why that way?"

"In case Susan is up. What we're doing is none of her business."

The Gate of the Dead

The glow of the full moon outlined the canopy of palm trees behind Papa's house. Beds of fragrant flowers lined the stone path to the servant's quarters.

Carol whispered, "Could Papa have been kidding us about a map?"

"I don't know. We'll soon find out, I guess."

The servant's entrance door opened easily, and the light from an antique fixture left a strange pattern on the walls. Worn-out oak boards creaked underfoot as we approached the narrow attic stairway.

Gripping the wood railing, I prayed with each step it wouldn't give way.

At the top of the landing, I paused at the door. My pulse quickened as my sweaty hand gripped the dented brass doorknob and cracked it open. The darkness was unsettling. I entered and glanced around. There was a thin ribbon of light from under a window shade; a heavy damp, musty smell filled the room.

Carol protested. "I'm not going in there. It's too dark."

I pointed at the light coming from the window. "See, there's light," then took her hand and tried to pull her in. She resisted.

"Don't be a wuss, Carol. Remember when something frightened us Papa would quote Franklin Delano Roosevelt, 'We have nothing to fear but fear itself.' Be brave. When we find the map, we'll be very rich!"

She tugged at her gloves and ventured into the room.

Something grazed my cheek. I screamed, "Dear God!" and jumped back.

"What's the matter, Joel?"

"Something touched my face!" Feeling around in the air, my fingers felt a string. I pulled it, and a bulb went on.

She laughed, "Big brave brother scared of a string!"

"Very funny."

The bulb flickered, giving a creepy cast to a table laden with small dust-covered boxes. On one side of the table, trunks were lined up like soldiers. Each had a number on it, ranging from 1096–1680.

Leaning against the wall was an oil portrait of a woman in a big, gold, ornate frame that had an uncanny resemblance to Carol. On closer inspection, there was a small brass plate, engraved with the name, "Doña Catalina."

"Carol—she looks just like you—maybe she's a long-lost relative?"

The worn wooden floor flexed as we walked about.

Suddenly, Carol stopped, flailed her arms about and screamed, "Oh my God! Get it off me!"

"It's a cobweb. Now come on, let's go."

Brushing it from her face, Carol stomped her foot. A floorboard popped up and hit her in the nose.

"I'm bleeding—I'm bleeding!" She was hysterical. Blood flowed from her nose.

I held out a handkerchief—she snatched it, put it to her nose, squeezed her nostrils together, and threw her head back.

The blood dripped onto the floor, reminding me once again of *Carol beaten-up, lying in the woods.*

My attention was drawn to the space beneath the floorboard. A small wooden chest glared at me from its tomb.

Carol fidgeting and still holding her nostrils closed, watched as I crouched down and gingerly lifted the chest.

She mumbled, "What's that?"

"I don't know. It looks hundreds of years old."

"I don't care if it's old as Methuselah. Just take it, and let's get out of here."

"No, I want to see …"

"My nose hurts. Let's go."

"Hang in, I'll put it on the table and see what we've got. I promise it won't take long."

A small key dangled from a frayed, leather handle. I inserted the key in the padlock, tilted the lid back. Revealing a scroll and a map, I removed them and placed the scroll and map on the table, and carefully unrolled the parchment.

Carol stepped closer.

"Careful, we don't want to get blood on it," I warned.

I proceeded to read,

> *In a place that was there before the beginning*
> *Find the governor who points the way*
> *To the gate of the dead*
> *Over the hill that brave men dread*
> *Then the 1680 key will lead you to the greatest treasure in history*

I looked at my sister. "It's the map's key, but I don't understand it. The professor may be able to help."

Papa's Secret

The next morning, Carol and I were having an early breakfast when the phone rang, it was Professor Arenofsky. He said that Papa had instructed him that upon his death, he was to give us something of importance; and we must come immediately to his room at the Casa Monica Hotel.

Stunned and perplexed, as we prepared to leave, we decided to take the chest with us. We will have an opportunity to discuss its contents.

שׁשׁשׁ

As we drove, Carol hugged the chest as if someone might try to steal it.

We circled the Plaza de la Constitución and pulled into valet parking at the Casa Monica Hotel. Although the ornate Moorish-style lobby is like stepping into the sixteenth century, the matronly woman behind the registration, counter was definitely contemporary.

"What room is Professor Arenofsky in?" I inquired.

"Is he expecting you?"

"Yes."

"And your name, sir?

Carol answered. "We're the Schwartz's."

She looked at a computer screen. "He's in Suite 316."

When the elevator door opened, at the third floor, the professor's voice echoed. "Over here, over here ..."

There he was down the hall, waving to us.

It was a beautiful suite. Blue and gold satin drapes adorned a large concave window. A blue velvet sofa, two facing gold wingback chairs, a replica of an antique desk, and a chair in front of the window completed the scene.

The professor cleared his throat, stroked his short beard, and pointed to the sofa. "Please children, have a seat. I have urgent news."

Carol, still hugging the chest tightly, gave me a darting gaze.

The professor pulled a wingback chair over, sat down, leaned in, and continued. "Your father and I were more than just partners. We were like brothers, confiding our inner thoughts and feelings. He trusted me to turn his secret over to you if he should die before me.

"Joel, he told me that you and Carol slept in the same room. However, he also realized that he might have jumped to the wrong conclusion. I tried to get him to reconcile with the two of you, but I was unable to."

Carol sighed—I was dumbfounded!

"When we were making our plans for a late dinner the following night, he finally agreed to call you in the morning to apologize for his behavior."

Carol interjected, "When we were at the hospital, we were told that he had forgiven us, that his depraved thoughts about us were unfounded."

"But professor, why are we here?" I asked. The professor leaned forward. "Your father spent half his life researching the Kabbalah, and in the process, discovered that the passage *Pe'ulat ha-ko ah* is the key to changing time."

"That's crazy!" Carol blurted.

I poked her, and under my breath said, "Let him continue."

The professor leaned back in his chair and rubbed his goatee. "Let me explain. All time exists concurrently. Your father found that it's possible to change the time you're in, but not your location."

Carol shrugged. "I still don't get it."

"If you're standing on a bridge, and change to a period prior to the bridge being built, you would find yourself in midair, and immediately fall into the water."

Solemnly, he went on. "Scripture tells us that only the high priests of Israel, a Kohen, can pronounce **His** name and live. Therefore, only a Kohen can summon the power of the *Ten Sefirot*.

"By speaking God's name, a Kohen will receive the power to change time." He stroked his beard again.

"Your father was a pure Kohen, a direct descendant of Aaron and the House of David."

"What does that have to do with us?" Carol asked.

"Your father went back in time and traced Aaron's breastplate to 1702 Spanish, St. Augustine.

The breastplate gives the wearer direct communication with God."

I was speechless and just stared at him.

"Unfortunately, he suffered a heart attack before he could disclose where it was hidden. Now, that he's passed away, it means that you, Joel, are next in line to recover it."

I was numb. "Me, why me?"

"You have the power."

The Relic: Jerusalem to St. Augustine

"I don't have *any* extraordinary powers!"

"You do. You're just not aware of them."

Carol gave a nervous laugh. "You've got to be kidding! Papa must have been playing a joke. He always teased us when we were little."

The professor spoke directly to Carol, "No, I'm not kidding. This is very real."

She retorted, "It's ridiculous! It could never happen! Time travel is for sci-fi fans. It's totally impossible!"

The professor persisted. "Carol, you've heard of Nostradamus, who was a Kohen, a Kabbalist, and a physician?

"Yes, so?"

"He was able to change his time dimension and write about things he actually witnessed. Your father discovered the Kabbala's secret of time and told me he hid it in the attic. I looked and found nothing."

I took the chest from Carol, opened it, and removed the map and scroll. "This is what we found under the floorboards."

"May I examine them?"

"Of course."

After examining the contents, he concluded that he could not add anything to our discovery. Before we left, he insisted we keep in touch with him, especially if we learned anything new. We promised we would. He returned the map and scroll to me, and continued, "The last thing your father told me was to give you an envelope. He said it contained God's sacred name."

He unlocked the desk drawer, took out an envelope, and held it at arm's length as if it was on fire. Beads of perspiration ran down his face.

His voice quivered. "I'm not a Kohen. Here, Joel, take it."

He took a handkerchief from his jacket breast pocket, wiped his brow, and sighed in relief, "Know this: there are national and international entities, religious powers, which will stop at nothing to use what is in this envelope."

Had the professor lost his mind? I had no idea, but-but I'd play along.

He took from his pants pocket, two red-knotted strings, each about seven inches long, and handed one to Carol, the other to me.

"These are *Rachel's Red Strings*. For centuries, the string granted protection to the one who wore it."

Carol looked carefully at it, and asked, "How is that possible?"

The professor's face tensed. "Hashem protects anyone who wears it. Tie the one you have on your brother's left wrist, and Joel, do the same to your sister."

As I tied the red string on Carol's wrist, I said, "Professor, even if we could go back to the 1700s, in Spanish Florida, neither of us speaks Spanish."

"God can give you the power to speak and understand all languages."

Having discharged his obligations, took a deep breath, focused his eyes on us, raised his hands over our heads, and said, "Please bow your heads and repeat this prayer, *Ayin alei porat ben Yosef porat ben yivarech ra mikol oti hagoel hamalach shmi bahem vyikare han'arim et vYitzchak Avraham avotai vshem.* This prayer ensures God's protection. You may now raise your heads.

You must know that your father worked with the Mossad, Israel's secret service."

The Mossad! Dear God, what's he going to tell us next?

"Your father's wish is that you finish his mission by contacting Ben Amie." He handed me a white business card.

My mind was spinning like a pinwheel. *Had the professor lost his mind? Could this possibly be the truth?*

Who is this mysterious Mossad agent? What kind of secret mission could it be?

The Mossad

In the hotel's café, we sat at a table, placed the chest on it, and called Ben Amie's number on my cell phone.

A woman answered. "Good afternoon, Cohen Brothers LLC, International Food Distributors, may I help you?"

"Yes. I'm Joel Schwartz."

"We've been expecting your call. You are to meet Ben Amie tomorrow at 10 a. m. in St Augustine, at the Barnes & Noble Café."

"How will I recognize him?"

"He's young and will be wearing a red, white, and blue T-shirt with the American flag on the back. He'll be drinking a latte and working on the New York Times crossword puzzle."

"Thank you."

I was ready to hang up when the voice continued. "One more thing. You're to ask, 'Did you finish the puzzle? He'll answer, 'Only 23 down is open.' Do you have any questions?"

"No."

"Thanks for calling." She hung up.

Carol asked, "Well, what did they say?"

"I'll explain in the car."

ששש

Thoughts of Ben Amie and the chest kept me up most of the night. Still bleary-eyed after breakfast, I locked the chest in the trunk of the car, and we left to find our destiny.

By the time we arrived at Barnes and Noble, I was fully awake. The Café's air was filled with an undercurrent of muted sounds: university students, people on cell phones, and a man and woman chatting over coffee.

But, no Ben Amie.

Carol grabbed my arm, pointed to a young man sitting in the corner. He was wearing a T-shirt with the American flag on the back.

"That must be him," she whispered.

We moved in close enough to see him working on the New York Times crossword puzzle.

We approached the side of his chair, "Excuse me, sir ..."

He immediately put down his pencil and looked up at us.

"Did you finish?" I asked.

"Not quite, only twenty-three down is open. Are you Joel Schwartz?"

"Yes, and this is my sister, Carol."

"Good to meet the both of you. Please sit down."

"Are you Ben Amie?"

His eyes scrutinized us. "Well, yes and no."

"What do you mean?"

"Ben Amie is a fictitious name. Call me, Josh."

I said, "Go on."

He continued. "I am going to tell you what your father was doing for us. He insisted we return Aaron's Breastplate to Israel. The relic gives the wearer God's power."

"That's not logical—it's superstitious nonsense.

"No, it's not. Your father traced the breastplate's journey, from 1193, during the third crusade when Spain's King Phillip II brought the Breastplate to Spain from Jerusalem. It remained there until the Inquisition, when it was smuggled out of Spain to Baracoa, Cuba, by Converses Count Abarbanel and Christopher Columbus.

Two-hundred years later, the breastplate, along with a chest of gold, was stolen by the Sword of Islam—the El-Kahattab. The El-Kahattab's ship was captured by elements of the Spanish Armada. The breastplate, along with the gold, was brought to the Spanish fortress in St Augustine for safekeeping. It remained there until the 1702 Queen Anne War, involving England, France, and Spain. Gov. James Moore, of English South Carolina, invaded St. Augustine, burned the town down, killed men, women, and children—then withdrew before a Spanish relief fleet could arrive from Cuba."

Carol's red string showed over the edge of her glove. She fingered it as she asked, "What does that have to do with us?"

"Until November 1702, Aaron's Breastplate and the chests of gold were kept under guard at the Treasury building.

Your father learned that during the early part of the raid, the breastplate with the gold was removed from the Treasury building and hidden somewhere in St. Augustine. He died without revealing where. You are the only known surviving male, who is also of the Davidic line and a Kohen, who can time travel. Joel, if you are willing to go back to the year 1702, recover the breastplate, and turn it over to us, you can keep the gold. We want only the breastplate. You will ensure peace for Israel. But, be forewarned: Going back in time could be very dangerous. We will not be able to assist you until you have returned to the present time!"

Carol interjected, "Excuse me, but if Joel is the only survivor of the House of David and also a Kohen, then what good would it do for the Arabs to possess the relic?"

"The New Testament, in Matthew 9:27, tells us that Jesus was from the House of David. Therefore, it is plausible there are Christian and Islamic branches of the Davidic line from the region during that time.

I know it's a lot to process, but the reality is that all of humanity could be affected by your decision."

I was dumbfounded. "We'll think about it and get back to you."

שׁשׁשׁ

The Mossad, Aaron's breastplate, could it be true? No, impossible! Oh shit, I don't know. Can all of humankind be depending on us?

I took a calming breath before starting the car, used my cell phone to call the professor, and told him we were on our way to discuss the meeting we just had with Ben Amie.

All the while, Carol sat rubbing the red string on her wrist.

Ms. Krief

On our way through the Casa Monica lobby, I noticed a tall, redheaded woman.

"That could be Ms. Krief," I said to Carol. "Let's follow her."

"You're as crazy as the professor." She added with a long sigh, "Joel, we don't have time for this."

"It bothers me. I have to find out if it's her."

At the reception desk, instead of telling the desk clerk to announce our presence to Professor Arenofsky, I said, "I'm looking for Ms. Krief; I'm supposed to meet her here, in the lobby."

"Ms. Krief, oh, yes—the tall, pretty lady." "Yes, that's her." I needed more information. "Are you sure she didn't go back up to her room, on the fourth floor?"

"I don't know, but, her suite is on the third floor."

We stepped away and made our way to the elevator.

"See Carol, it was her. Do you think it's a coincidence the professor and Ms. Krief are on the same floor?"

She shrugged. "What difference does it make?

שׁשׁשׁ

The professor questioned us, hung on our every word. He concluded there was nothing he could add. As we left, he insisted we keep in touch with him, especially if we learned anything new.

I suggested to Carol that we find a bench in the city plaza, and try to figure out what was going on, particularly the riddle of the Breastplate, and where it and the gold could be hidden.

Between the plaza and the Bridge of Lions is a vehicular turnabout, with a raised concrete base, supporting a life-size statue of Ponce de Leon, pointing north towards the Castillo.

We sat on a park bench facing the statue

"This cloak-and-dagger stuff is ridiculous," she said, "Doctor Schwartz; it's time you put that photographic memory of yours to work."

"In a place that was there before the beginning

Find the governor who points the way

To the gate of the dead

Over the hill that brave men dread

Then the 1680 key, will lead you to the greatest treasure in history

"So, big brother with the Ph.D., what does it all mean?"

"What can be 'before the beginning?"

"Beats me." She fumbled around in her pocketbook.

"What are you looking for in there?"

She held up her sunglasses, "These," then clumsily dropped them.

Automatically I reached over to pick them up; and at that exact moment, what sounded like a bullet, whizzed over my head.

As I pulled Carol to the ground, I caught a glimpse of a fleeting sightseeing horse-drawn carriage. The driver's long red hair blew in the wind.

"Carol, don't move."

"What are you doing?"

Déjà vu, we were back in the woods. I was standing over her, repeating the same words, "Carol, don't move ...."

Carol's face drained of color, "Joel, let's go home. The professor knows what he's talking about! Whoever shot at us will do anything to get what they want."

A green and orange tour trolley stopped in front of us. The tour guide's amplified voice blasted, 'On your left is a statue of Ponce de Leon. He accompanied Columbus on his second voyage. He also received an appointment as Governor of

Hispaniola. He's most noted for claiming Florida for Spain in 1513,' " and then the trolley went on its way.

Carol was quiet as we drove to Papa's house. Walking up the pathway, she fussed with the knots on her red string.

שׁשׁשׁ

"Joel, how did they find out so fast?

The next morning, I found Carol in the kitchen picking at a bagel. "My God you look like hell!" she rattled.

"Thanks much." I poured myself a cup of coffee.

Carol broke the silence, "We need a break, clear out the cobwebs. Let's go sailing, like when we were kids. I'll bring our favorite lunch. Catch my drift?"

We laughed.

שׁשׁשׁ

Papa kept his boat at the marina next to the Vilano Bridge. We arrived as the sun peeked over the horizon

The Relic: Jerusalem to St. Augustine

An old sailors' saying came to mind, *Red skies at night, sailors delight. Red sky in the morning, sailors take warning.*

The slapping of small waves against the wooden dock, sent droplets toward my legs as we stood next to Papa's old forty-eight-foot catamaran. It made an impressive sight.

Setting sail, we ventured far out beyond sight of land, tacking for hours across the moderate swells.

We dropped sail, and I threw over a mooring line that trailed behind.

"I'm going for a dip, Carol."

She popped her head out of the galley. "Fine, just don't drown."

"Very funny," then dove in from the stern, and grabbed the mooring line. The cool ocean calmed my sweltering body. I turned onto my back, closed my eyes, and let the rhythms of the drift relax me, while the sun played hide and seek among the clouds. Papa's words came to mind, *A place that was there before the beginning. Find the governor, who points the way to the gate of the dead,*' It hit me, *Papa was a genius—the simplicity. Papa knew my love for American history would provide the key to his message.*

Purplish-gray thunderheads closed in; waves swelled; the whitecaps increased, tossing me around as if to swallow me.

Through the turbulence came the whirling sound of a helicopter trying to hover over us.

The Coast Guard must be searching for stragglers in trouble, thank God help is here. Then I saw someone with long red hair aiming a rifle at me from the cockpit!

A pop—a splash—next to me! Adrenaline kicked in. I let go of the mooring line, swam underwater to the ladder, against the starboard side.

Carol screamed hysterically, "Joel, are you all right?" The helicopter sped away.

Papa's compass wasn't working—wouldn't you know it—the heavy cloud cover made it impossible to read the sky. We were too far out to see the land. That redheaded bitch actually saved our lives, because the chopper had to be heading back to land.

We sailed in the same direction. When we reached the shore, I called the Sheriff's Office. "I was shot at by a red-headed woman in an unmarked helicopter. I believe it was a Ms. K-R-I-E-F, a journalist from the local newspaper."

There was a considerable delay, and my anger grew as I waited. Just as I was about to hang up, an officer got on the call and identified himself.

"Sir, all inquiries about her will be relayed to the FBI, and they will contact you."

שׁשׁשׁ

I'd spent another sleepless night consumed with Papa's words when it finally dawned on me. How simple it was. "I've got it! I've got it!" I shouted.

Carol called, "What did you say? I'm just getting out of the shower."

Hollering back up the hallway, I cried, "I've got it! "I know where the gate of the dead is! The statue of Ponce de Leon is pointing north."

"So?" Carol said, coming to the door and peeking her head out at me.

"Think! Ponce de Leon was the governor of Hispaniola, before the founding of St. Augustine in 1565. Therefore, all we have to do is follow the direction the statue is pointing, to find the gate of the dead."

"I still don't get it."

"The old walled city was only two blocks wide. We can follow the bayfront north from the plaza, or we can start from the old Government House and follow St. George Street."

Carol's eyes, widened. "Which do we try first?"

"We could start at the statue at the bayfront, on San Marco Avenue."

"We could."

I shook my head. "No. On second thought, that's too obvious. Papa was much too clever. Because of his reference to the governor; we should start at the

Government House, where the Spanish governors ran the city."

"I'm impressed, brother dear. But what if you're wrong?"

"We'll try San Marco on the Bayfront."

שׁשׁשׁ

It was late morning when we stood under the balcony of the Government House, map, and clues in hand.

Carol remarked, "I hope no one shoots at us today."

"Not funny," I snapped.

"I wasn't trying to be funny," she said.

"Carol, focus on finding what could be the gate of the dead."

I pointed north, in the same direction indicated by the Ponce de Leon statue.

Crossing the street, Carol exclaimed, "Look! The Cathedral has two gates!"

"Hmm, interesting. However, we're not looking for two gates."

"Okay."

A few feet beyond the Cathedral was the Woman's Exchange and in front a sign that read,

The Peña-Peck House, Circa 1750, By Order Of the King of Spain as the Residence of His Royal Treasurer, Juan Esteban De Peña.

Carol said, "Look. The old Spanish treasurer's house has a gate."

"The last line of the puzzle will lead you to the greatest treasure in history; treasure and treasurer—that could make sense."

"Let's take a look."

We entered through the gate, into the peaceful, walled garden where bougainvillea showed off its beautiful deep pink flowers.

It was easy to visualize early residents sitting beneath the shade of the giant live oak tree or in the loges on rainy, humid, summer evenings.

After meandering around, and not finding a grave, we continued along St. George Street to Hypolita Street.

The Relic: Jerusalem to St. Augustine

There's a small fenced-in garden, called the Hispanic Gardens.

A bronze sculpture depicts Spain's Queen Isabella on a donkey, being led down a hill.

A few feet behind her is a grape arbor that runs the entire width of. the property.

We searched, to no avail. I was frustrated.

After walking a few more blocks, Carol poked me, tilted her chin up, shifted her eyes upward and whispered, "Don't look"—it was difficult for me not to. "I think it's Ms. Krief watching us."

Close by was the silhouette of a red rooster jutting out from a small, white-stucco building, with a sign, painted in white *Taberna del Gallo*, (Tavern of the Rooster), ca. 1734. "Carol, Let's duck into that tavern."

Its decor was right out of the 1700's. A rough wood bar stood out against a white stucco wall. Pewter and ceramic mugs hung from the ceiling.

We sat at a wood plank table and stared out the window waiting to see if Ms. Krief would pass by.

A man behind the bar, dressed as an 18th-century sailor, called out, in a New York accent, "Either of yaw wants a beer or sangria?"

I responded, "Two sangrias, please."

"Are yaw, waiting for someone?

"No!"

We stared out the window for what seemed a long time, when a redheaded woman walked by.

Carol sighed. "It's not her."

I closed my eyes for a moment, *Thank God.* "Come. Let us continue the search."

Part II

All things are possible with God.

Mark 10:27

1680

We followed St. George Street, north, to the old City Gate.

Carol's face reflected my disappointment. She placed her hand on one of the majestic coquina columns, which bracketed the only entrance to the walled city. I walked over and put my arm around her.

"We'll have to start over again at the bayfront."

She started to walk away, turned back to the columns, and gave the area one last look.

Then a revelation showed on her face. "Joel come here," she said, pointing a finger. "Look, between the columns."

I did, wondering, *what is she looking at?*

She continued, "On the other side of the street if memory serves me correctly, that's the stone wall of an old cemetery."

"You're right. Let's take a look."

Sure enough, on the arch above the wrought-iron gate were the words, Huguenot Cemetery. *Could this be the Gate of The Dead?*

I immediately recalled Papa's story about the ghost of John B. Stickney, which had repeatedly been seen in that graveyard since 1882.

Turning full circle from the gate, keeping in mind what could be the *'Over the hill that brave men dread,'* it dawned on me, "That's it!"

"That's what?"

"Over the hill that brave men dread!" I snatched her hand and led her across the street.

"Are you're sure? How do you know?"

We stood on the bottom of the hill that fronted the Castillo de San Marcos.

"Carol this has to be the hill that brave men dread."

"What do you mean?"

"Observe the Castillo's bastions. The cannons are facing us from three sides. Surviving an attack from this direction would be impossible. This has to be the hill that brave men dread."

"You are a genius! However, without the last line, it all leads to naught! Now figure out the last line."

"You're right. But I'm hungry, let's get some pizza."

שׁשׁשׁ

I couldn't sleep that night, my mind replaying the words, '*Then the 1680 key.*' Around three in the morning, my exhaustion won.

The morning sun awakened me. *What if the key is not a key?* The thought kept turning in my mind as I stepped from

The Relic: Jerusalem to St. Augustine

the shower. The steamy water not only opened my pores but also my brain. I said the line '1680 key' backward several times.

Eureka! It's not a physical key. I nearly slipped getting out of the shower, wrapped a towel around me, ran into Carol's bedroom; and shouted, "Carol, the 1680 key is not a key, at all, but a point in time—a year! Papa wants us to go to 1680."

"You're dripping on me!" she shrieked—pulling the blanket up to her neck. "What do we do now?"

My photographic memory evoked the old trunk with "1680" on it. "We are going to the attic."

"Are you putting on some clothes first?" she asked with one eyebrow arched.

"Sure. Meet me at the attic door in five minutes."

ששש

When I opened the attic door, Carol sneezed repeatedly. "My eyes are running. I'm not going any further," she insisted.

"We have to find the key to the treasure. We'll be super rich." I handed her my handkerchief to wipe her eyes. "Take a deep breath and come on."

She stepped across the threshold breathing through the handkerchief. "Be careful of the loose floorboard," she murmured through the cloth.

I went straight for the light bulb string. The bulb illuminated the room. Spotting the trunk marked 1680, my skin tingled, and my senses heightened.

Carol complained, "Damn these cobwebs, Joel," and then became quiet when she too saw, 1680 on a trunk

ששש

Dust flew as I opened the lid.

Carol coughed, "Good God, Joel—it's only old clothes."

Rummaging through, it quickly became apparent everything was there, even Spanish coins that we would need. I held up an elaborately patterned brocade dress. "Look, Carol, you can wear this."

The Relic: Jerusalem to St. Augustine

She sneezed and sniffled, "God only knows who wore that. Be careful, it may fall apart."

She came closer and gingerly took it from me. Holding it at arm's length, she seemed a bit less upset at the idea. "I'm surprised it doesn't smell. It's amazing it's in such good condition. Do you realize, Joel, this is a Mantua style dress …?"

"What do I know about Mantua style? Or even care?" I said returning my search to the trunk.

"It's slenderizing," she said.

"Carol, you impress me with your knowledge."

"What are you going to wear, my dear brother?"

Rummaging deep into the chest, I pulled out a brown waistcoat.

It had red ribbon loops on the shoulders that held attached sleeves, and matching breeches, a white button-less shirt, long white stockings, and a red-heeled pair of shoes.

As we left, I expressed my impression that the oil painting of Doña Catalina bore an uncanny resemblance to Carol. She laughed.

"People will think we've lost our minds walking around dressed in these clothes."

"No," I said. "We'll blend right in with the fort's re-enactors in the morning."

She shrugged off her hesitation. "Yeah. I suppose."

Castillo

After breakfast, I went to my room and Carol to hers. I put on my 17th-century outfit, and before I could check myself out in the mirror, Carol called out.

"Joel the dress is heavy and ..."

"I'll be right there."

Standing in her bedroom doorway, I watched Carol admire herself in a full-length oval mirror.

"Carol, you're absolutely pulchritudinous."

"What exactly does that mean, Dr. Joel?

"Beautiful."

The Rachel-red string peeked out from her white glove. She smiled, tugged at the glove, and said, "Thanks. Now what do we do, big shot?"

"That's easy. We'll hide on the second floor of the English barracks.

"Why there?"

"It's closed to the public; we'll stay there until the fort closes, then we'll go out to the green, and back to 1680.

"I don't know, Joel. What if it doesn't work?"

"Well, if there is a God, it'll be 1680. If not; we'll go back home when the fort opens in the morning."

As we approached the front door, Carol stopped and insisted, "I've to get another pair of my gloves, I'll be right back."

It took but a moment, and she handed them to me. "Here, put these in your backpack."

"Carol, nobody will be looking at your finger."

"Just put them in the pack!"

שׁשׁשׁ

The day seemed sharply real and not real at all.

"Carol, remember what Bubba used to say, 'If you have a choice to be rich, pretty, or lucky, choose lucky.' Today we're lucky."

"Why lucky?"

"See, over there, by the Castillo's entrance, there's a group of re-enactors."

"Yes."

"They're ready to enter the fort. Come, let's mingle." Grasping her hand, off we charged.

שׁשׁשׁ

Excitement, anticipation, and fear soared all at once, as we crossed over the drawbridge to the green. Once on the other side, we separated from the group and entered the English barracks next to the chapel.

Carol pointed to the bunk beds against the wall and whispered, "Judging from the size of these beds, the people must have been very short in those days."

Toward the rear of the room, wooden steps led up to the second floor, our intended hiding place. All we needed now was an opportunity to sneak up the stairs unnoticed.

A National Park Service ranger walked to the center of the green, and bellowed, "There will be a live demonstration of a 1740s cannon drill and firing, on the gun deck."
I stood in the doorway and watched the volunteer re-enactors, dressed in Spanish military uniforms, parade around the green. They stopped in front of the stone steps that lead to the terreplein.

This is it! "Carol there's our diversion. While everyone follows the cannon crew up to the gun deck, we go unnoticed to the second floor of the barracks."

The second floor was a duplicate of the first. The air was stuffy. We sat on the edge of a bunk bed.

It wasn't long before a ranger announced that the fort would be closing in fifteen minutes.

Carol was nervous and scared. "Joel, It's getting dark in here. It's spooky."

"It'll be all right, just take a deep breath, and exhale slowly."

Thinking that it might help reduce the tension, I hummed while fumbling in the knapsack for the flashlight. All it did was annoy Carol.

"Stop that humming,"

I stopped, and then flicked on the flashlight. The thin beam of light made things even creepier.

"Oh God, Joel ..."

Grasping her sweaty hand, I urged, "Carol it's time to go."

"I'm scared."

"Take deep breaths. You'll be alright."

"I don't feel good," she moaned. "My legs feel funny," she complained, as we slowly made our way down the creaky wooden steps to the first floor.

Before we ventured out, I turned off the flashlight and put it on the wooden table.

"Joel, what the hell are you doing? We need the light!"

"Carol keep your voice down. How would we explain a flashlight to people in 1680? Look, there's enough light coming through the veil of clouds. It'll be alright,"

"God, it's weird, like walking in a graveyard."

I held her hand tightly. "Keep quiet and walk."

We climbed the stone steps by feeling our way against the rough coquina wall. "Carol, if there is a God, it will work."

We approached a nearby watchtower and stopped. Placing the knapsack on the ground, "This is where we transmute."

"And if it doesn't work …?"

Stepping on her words, I whispered, "I promise we'll head back to New Jersey tomorrow."

There is a God!

I said the prayer aloud, with eyes shut and arms stretched toward heaven, and called out God's holy name to summon the Ten Sefirot to transmute us back to 1680.

Then, what felt like an electric bolt flowed down my arms and through my body. A brilliant full moon lit up the fort. Stars shimmered in the havens.

Carol screeched, "Wha … what happened? Let's get out of here, Joel."

Before we could do anything, footsteps echoed behind us, and a deep voice boomed, "Who goes there? Hands up!" A man in a 17th-century blue and red Spanish military uniform pointed his musket at us.

Carol seized my hand.

My voice trembled, "We were tired and hot and went inside to cool off."

He laughed, "You were tired and hot and went inside? Some story."

"It's true," Carol whimpered, squeezing my hand.

"Sure, sure," pointing his musket in the direction of a dirt ramp at the rear corner of the fort. 'Come on—walk," he ordered. "We'll let the commander decide what to do with the two of you. Now move!"

Carol hyperventilated and pulled at her gloves as we walked.

"Breathe slowly," I told her.

"Be quiet. Move!" The guard shouted, poking us with his musket.

I whispered, "Carol, we'll be alright." *Please God, don't let her faint.*

ששש

We walked through a long, narrow room off to the side of the Castillo entrance. An offensive odor emanated from the men sleeping shoulder to shoulder on one, long platform bed.

We continued walking into an adjoining room where a huge wooden door loomed before us.

In the middle of the door was a square hole, about the size of my head.

The guard held the musket in one hand while opening the door with the other, and ordered, "You'll spend the night in this cell."

He prodded me with the butt of his musket, causing me to stumble, pulling Carol down with me to the damp cell floor. The door closed.

Carol's hand tightened around mine. She coughed then whimpered "It's dark ...."

In the far a corner, a single lantern flickered, casting a narrow, uneven streak of light across the dirt floor.

ששש

Sitting on the damp dirt floor was miserable. Carol snuggled close. Our breathing echoed in the stagnant air.

My foremost–concern—what would happen if the soldiers found the Hebrew prayer? We'd be accused of being witches.

"What will become of us?" Carol whimpered.

Ignoring the question, I whispered, "We need to get rest."

"What's to become of us?"

I took out the parchment containing the prayer. "All I do know is that we've got to get rid of this."

"Why?"

"It's written in Hebrew!"

Carol went hysterical. "They'll kill us! Let's transmute to the 21st Century right now."

"Calm down, we have to let this play out. Remember Papa always preached, 'We must trust in Hashem. Remember the treasure Carol, the treasure."

She quieted, for the moment. Conflicted, she finally stuttered, "I guess."

The Relic: Jerusalem to St. Augustine

"It'll be alright. We know the prayer by heart. We don't need the parchment. I'll burn it in the lantern. If worse comes to worse, we can always transmute to the 21st Century."

It burnt quickly, into small ashes. Then Carol calmed herself, and we dozed.

שוש

I had no sense of time when we heard the sound of approaching boots.

"Joel …"

I put my fingers to my lips. "Shush …" and went over to the small opening in the cell door.

A man stood by the barrack archway dressed in a uniform with gold embroidery, and laden with medals. The soldiers scrambled to attention. He barked, "Bring the prisoners to me!"

Carol clung to me as the heavy door creaked open. My breathing intensified; my mouth was dry. We stepped out, walked a few feet when Carol's mouth fell open—"It's Papa!"

It blew my mind!

His familiar voice commanded, "No talking. Follow me."

There is a God! We did it! It's 1680, and our Papa is the commander of the Castillo in St. Augustine.

The Seventh Son
Of
The Seventh Son

The daylight hurt my eyes. Papa paused for a moment in the middle of the drawbridge. He wafted his hand through the air to punctuate his feelings, "This is wonderful. You can stay with me." Then we hurried off.

We walked on a dry and dusty dirt path alongside the earthen-and-log defense wall that surrounded the city. We passed some weary people and a couple of loaded wagons pulled by worn-out horses.

Carol tugged at her glove and sneezed repeatedly. On the settlement's main street were shops and wooden houses.

We stopped at a tabby wall with deep purple bougainvillea growing over it.

"We're here," Papa announced.

He opened the courtyard gate and gestured for us to enter.

The path crunched under our feet. On either side, a profusion of tropical flowers created a riot of color. The blossoms' sweet scent made my nose twitch: not far ahead, stood a small wooden one-story house with a flat roof.

We entered. *Yes, it was real.*

Hand-hewn cedar siding, open glassless windows with evenly spaced wooden bars. Papa boasted, "The only thing I bought is the brazier I use for cooking and heat in the winter."

He made an all-encompassing gesture. "I made all the rest."

On the far side of the room, a vase of flowers rested on a wooden table. Carol walked to it, pulled out the bench from beneath, and sat down.

Papa stroked his fingertips over the tabletop and proclaimed, "See how smooth it is?"

Mimicking him, she responded, "Smooth."

"Dear child, take off your gloves."

I did everything I could to keep from interfering. *After all these years, he would know better than to mention the gloves.*

Her eyes glistened with tears, but she smiled graciously.

With chest puffed, he went over to the colorful, overstuffed pillows on the floor. "My men's wives made them for me as a gift."

"And who cooks for you?"

"Why I do, of course!"

Papa making furniture—cooking!—sitting on the floor. It blew my mind.

He tilted his chin towards a three-sided wood box with a large round hole in the top, "See that?"

"What is it?" she asked.

"It contains a terracotta pot, to do your private business in."

She rolled her eyes.

Carol blurted out—"Papa, what the hell is going on?"

Papa walked over and embraced her, his voice faltering, "Please, Carol please, let me explain."

Her face reddened. "You're dead—but you're not dead?"

Papa's demeanor was calm, "We are Kohen's direct descendants of Aaron. I'm the seventh son in a line of seven sons. I'm able to live in two different time dimensions simultaneously. Because of my death in 2012, I will have to live out my life here."

Heavy with emotion, he turned to me. "Joel, because you are my first and only son—you can only be in one-time dimension at a time."

Carol and I were unable to say anything.

Papa's words flowed, "I wanted you to love God as I do; raising you as my father raised me and his father raised him."

The Relic: Jerusalem to St. Augustine

My old feeling of confrontation welled up within me.

Papa professed, "That is to obey Torah and its laws as interpreted by the Hasidic rabbis. I wanted the two of you to be a reflection of the Torah and myself."

Three uneven lines creased his forehead. Silence hung in the dead air for a moment.

"I'm not so perfect children; that day at your apartment, after you received your Ph.D., I opened your bedroom door by mistake."

Carol gasped, "Oh dear God, Papa!"

"I really thought the two of you were sleeping together. I excommunicated both of you from my life believing—if your behavior changed, God would forgive the two of you. And after enduring years of pain from our separation, I realized I had ruined all of our lives."

His shoulders slumped, his eyes filled with tears, "Please forgive me for my hardheaded stubbornness, so Hashem can forgive all three of us before we turn to dust."

"Papa, why are you here now?"

"Early in 1680, the local native Yemassee Indians revolted. They massacred a number of the settlers. At that time, the fort was only partially completed.

If the Yemasee overcame the fort, it would have changed history. I came here to prevent a historic paradigm shift."

"But why did you bring us here?" Carol asked.

"Come, let's sit."

We sat around the dining room table. Papa placed his fingers under his beard and rested his chin.

There was brooding about him as he spoke. "It all started years ago. Before retiring from the university, I discovered, the Kabbalah's secret of changing time dimensions, and used the secret exclusively for my academic research.

After retirement, I entered a partnership with my so-called lifelong friend, Ira Arenofsky."

"Why do you call him so-called?" I interrupted.

"I'm coming to that Joel, be patient." His smile was thin. "We went into the custom antiquities business. The agreement was since I am a Kohen who can call out God's name and change time dimensions, I'd secure the artifacts, and he, a Levy, would take care of the business end of things.

Joel, at the university we had contacts with museums and collectors from around the world.

Our business proliferated. We drew what monies we needed and invested the rest for us."

"Did you have a written contract?"

"No, just a handshake."

With that, I saw Carol's eyes dilate.

"What an illusion I was under! Thinking he was all wise."

"Joel, he was my best and oldest friend. I'm no good at legal and business matters, so I let him do it. Remember, we went to Yeshiva together. He was the best man at my wedding. I trusted him implicitly."

Carol exclaimed, "Oh, Papa!"

"I trusted him like a brother. He made out my will. He reassured me he'd take care of everything and that you and Carol would inherit my share of the business."

Papa's eyes turned hard. "I told Ira, I wanted to see my will. He suggested we have dinner at our favorite place and he would bring a copy with him."

He looked away, cleared his throat and then looked at us again. "At dinner, I excused myself to go to the men's room.

When I got back, the entrée was on the table. By the time dessert came, I was light-headed—then had acute stomach and chest pains. That's the last thing I remember."

"Oh my God, Papa, he poisoned you?"

Papa brought a cupped hand to his mouth and muttered, "No I don't think he would do that."

"So why are we here?' Carol asked again.

He composed himself and resumed. "Some years from now, on November 10,

1702, Col. James Moore will lead an English invasion of St. Augustine. He will burn the town down but will not overtake the fort.

"Treasury building records of early 1702 show that Aaron's Breastplate was kept in one of the two chests that held gold."

Carol and I stared at each other and simultaneously said, "Chest of gold!"

"During the raid, an engineer by the name of Juan Caruso, will remove and hide the treasure somewhere in St. Augustine. However, he died in a shipwreck a short time after, without disclosing its hiding place. Since I can no longer change time, the two of you must go to 1702. You are to locate and befriend Juan Caruso, find the treasure, and recover it for yourselves and take it back to the 21st Century."

1702

Before breakfast, we went to St. George St. and transmuted to November 5, 1702. It was a chilly, gusty, overcast morning.

"Joel I'm hungry," Carol declared.

I stopped a passerby to ask where we could eat.

He pointed, down the street, "*The Kings Inn*. The food's good there."

The Kings Inn sign hung from a white tabby building, with vines of jasmine that hugged its walls. Inside, aromas of baked bread, coffee, and tobacco mingled with the smell of unwashed bodies. Customers seated at tables stared at us and muttered. We made our way to a corner table.

A short, fat man waddled over to us. "Never seen the two of you around here before—are you visiting?"

Carol piped up, "Yes we are. Please take our order."

"Drink or food? What's your pleasure?"

"I'll have café con leche and a tarta. The lady will have the same." Then I added, "We're from Pensacola. We're looking for Señor Juan Caruso. Have you seen him?"

"Not recently!" He turned and walked away.

A man sitting alone at a table next to us turned. The lines in his weathered face; looked as if though they had been drawn with a black marker. Wiry black hairs stuck out in every direction from under his bandanna. Heavy tobacco odor accompanied his words.

"Looking for Juan Caruso, are yaw now?"

"Yes, Juan Caruso, the engineer, do you know him?"

"Yes, he is working on the watchtower. He lives in a cabin near there. He comes into town once every month for supplies. You just missed him. He was here only yesterday."

He turned away, picked his cup up, took a swig, turned back to us.

"Diego's the name. For only two silver reales I can row you over to the island. But it has to be today."

Who is this man? On the other hand, how dangerous can it be? Anastasia Island is only a few minutes directly across the bay.

ששש

We followed Diego to the bayfront. There, a small dinghy with a flat, square bow sat on a sand dune. Diego slid the boat partly into the water; gawked at Carol, then shouted, "Woman! Get in!"

Carol's hand trembled. With a tight voice, she started to say, "Joel ..."

I raised my hands to stop her. "Remember, 'There's nothing to fear but fear itself.' It'll be okay."

Carol tugged at her gloves and then stepped into the dinghy.

She squealed when the dingy tilted under her weight. Diego pushed the boat a bit farther into the bay; Carol jumped in and sat on the center seat.

He ordered me to push the dinghy further into the water until it was afloat,

"Okay get in." He ordered. I took the last seat, facing them both ignoring the water pouring off my boots.

Diego rowed out into the inlet. The swells grew in height and intensity. *Oh dear God! Davis Shores didn't exist until 1920. We'll have to go around Bird Island into the open sea.*

Carol grabbed the edges of the boat, and cried out, "I'm scared, and I'm getting soaked!"

The wind roared, and I shouted, "Diego, I will double your fee if you get us to shore immediately; anywhere will do."

He pulled hard on the right oar, the dinghy jerked left. As we lunged forward on a wave, Carol screamed again.

A few pulls of the oars, and we reached the shore.

Diego laughed, "This is what you wanted, sir." His demeanor suddenly changed.

With the seriousness of a tradesman, he extended a dirty, callused hand, palm up, "Four silver reales, now!"

I dropped the coins into his palm, and like a clamshell, his hand snapped closed.

He pointed a gnarled index finger. "The Watchtower is that way. Now, get out!"

We stood dripping wet on the shore as he blew a kiss to Carol, and rowed away.

Señor Juan Caruso

We walked along the ocean's edge. Sunlight glittered off the soft, hot sand. The marbled white clouds shaped themselves into puffs of cotton against the blue sky. Nearby a great white egret preened, an enormous turtle surfaced a few feet away, and Ibis fed on small crustaceans exposed by the ebbing tide. The intensity of the sun's heat and glare was nauseating. We needed to find shade.

It didn't take us long to reach a tree line with its carpet of dried leaves and pine needles. The canopy of majestic live oak made it cooler.

All kinds of bugs clung to us as we trudged through tightly packed twisted vines that scratched and chafed. It was a fatiguing obstacle course.

The dense woods forced us to walk single file. Carol's footsteps became fainter.

"Hurry, Carol," I shouted over my shoulder, "Be careful of the snakes and whatever else is in here."

She caught up to me in two minutes, her hair matted and tangled with leaves. Swatting insects away, with perspiration dripping down her neck, and gasping for breath, she asked, "What else is in here?"

"Wild boars, panthers, spiders the size of dinner plates."

"Who do you think we are Tarzan and Jane? This is crazy. Forget the treasure. I want to go back home, NOW!"

I felt the same way, but I knew we couldn't turn back. We had to go on.

"Joel this is insane!" she cried.

My voice denied my feelings as I said, "Where is your sense of adventure, Carol?"

She tugged at her gloves and sobbed, "Sense of adventure? We could be killed!"

I put my arm around her shoulders and empathized. "We can go back and follow the beach around the island."

"But the heat …."

"We'll be ok." She composed herself, and so we left the god-forsaken jungle.

We plodded over the hot sand, neither of us uttering a word, as sweat poured from our every pore, making our clothing even more burdensome. My breathing became labored, and after a while; all my muscles quivered.

When I thought I couldn't take another step, Carol called out, "A boat."

I wiped the sweat from my eyes, and there, in the distance, near the water's edge, was the silhouette of a small boat under a lonely palm tree. A surge of adrenaline shot through my body. I grabbed Carol's arm, and we ran as fast as we could towards it.

When we reached the boat, I collapsed in the palm tree's shadow, rested my back against the boat, and closed my eyes. Carol crouched down and wanted know if I was all right.

I managed to utter, "I'm fine."

"No, you're not. You look pale. Let me take your pulse."

She took off her gloves.

"It's elevated but regular. You just need some rest."

Exhausted, I fell asleep, for how long I don't know.

ʊʊʊ

Carol shook me awake. "You look much better."

Carol now enthused, continued. "I saw the watchtower. We must be close to Juan Caruso's cabin and the treasure. Come on—let's go." She dashed ahead, holding her skirts tightly in her hands.

My legs were still rubbery. By the time, I reached the edge of the woods;

The Relic: Jerusalem to St. Augustine

Carol was out of sight. *How could she disappear so quickly?* Dark memories of years ago rushed back.

Carol in the woods, lying curled up and bleeding, the screeching of the birds, her finger, the blood. No, I am not going to let it happen again!

I entered the jungle canopy screaming, repeating, "Carol, where the hell are you?"

Then I saw her. She was standing, frozen, up against a tree, her face colorless.

Through clenched teeth, she cried out, "Joel stop—don't move!"

A wild boar, snorting angrily, circled the tree. *Boars are killers—please God don't let anything happen to her.*

The boar lowered its massive head, snorted, front legs kicking up dirt. Then his tank-like body with two razor-sharp tusks charged at Carol.

She let out a blood-curdling shriek. I closed my eyes knowing it would be over in seconds.

From out of nowhere, a loud explosion thundered. I opened my eyes—there, only inches from her, lay the boar—motionless on its side.

As I ran to her, a forceful, voice boasted, "That was a close one."

A man who looked like a nobleman in woodsman's clothing emerged with a smoking musket cradled in one arm.

Carol's knees buckled as she leaned into me.

He shifted his intense, deep-set eyes to Carol.

"And who are you my pretty one?"

Speechless, her tears welled up.

"No tears, please." He removed his hat, bowed, and said, "I'm Señor Juan Caruso." He replaced his hat, then turned away, and poked at his prize with his musket.

"Please call me Juan. And you are?"

"I'm Joel, and this is my sister Carol."

He let out a hearty laugh, "I thought this beautiful lady was your wife."

"Sir, we have come a long way to see you."

He became serious. "Why me?"

"Please, we need to talk to you."

He looked at the boar, then at us. "My cabin is close by. I'll come back later for the carcass." He reloaded his musket and motioned, "Follow me."

We followed him along a well-defined path to his cabin. Juan opened the door and extended an arm, in welcome. We were astonished to see such a spacious room with bookcases on either side of a huge, stone fireplace. Positioned on the mantel, blue-and-white candlesticks flanked a portrait of a woman.

Closer inspection revealed books titled in Spanish, French, English, and Greek. To the right, was a highly polished wood dining table enough to accommodate ten people. In the center sat a silver tray with a crystal decanter of wine, and matching goblets. The décor's sophistication was in sharp contrast to the log walls.

שׁשׁשׁ

Please have a seat," Juan said, as he poured the wine. "Enjoy. I noticed you were staring at my books."

"Yes. I see they are in various languages."

"I was educated at universities in England and Spain."

Carol lifted her glass for a sip of wine, the red string at her wrist slipped out from under her glove.

Juan cleared his throat, "I don't mean to be rude, but is that a Rachel's-red string on your wrist?"

"Yes, our Papa left one to each of us."

He held out his hand like a stop signal. "You do know what a Converso is?"

"Why?"

He went on, "My Spanish heritage dates back to the 1200s when Jews were encouraged to migrate to Spain to help build the country's economic base. Throughout the reign of Ferdinand and Isabella, a relative named Count Arbarbanel, the Treasurer of Spain, arranged the financing for Columbus's first voyage in 1492.

The Spanish Inquisition, which began, in 1476, forced all non-Catholics to convert to Christianity. Most Jews left Spain. Those who stayed publicly converted, but continued to practice Judaism in secret.

My family made the risky decision to become Converso and was thus able to maintain their economic and social standing. The Inquisition pressed the search for those who pretended to practice Christianity."

Carol asked, "How did they find out who was not really a Christian?"

"They used torture until those suspected admitted they were Jews. It was quite horrible."

She pressed on. "What kind of torture?"

"I do not speak of such atrocities in front of a woman." Changing the subject, he turned to me.

"Joel, we can't leave the boar—we have to retrieve it before predators get to it."

He jumped to his feet, smiled at Carol, "You will stay here. Rest—we shall not be long."

Juan and I went behind the cabin to retrieve the travois and set out for the boar.

שׁשׁשׁ

On our way to retrieve the boar, my curiosity got the best of me. "What kind of torture did the Spanish use?" I asked.

His voice dropped a pitch, "The *strappado*."

"The what?"

We stopped, and he enunciated as if I was hard of hearing. "*STRAPPADO*, *strappado*, it is simple.

The victim's hands are tied behind his back, and then he is suspended in the air using a rope attached to the wrists."

"Good God, their shoulders must dislocate!"

"That's not the half of it. Weights were added to the feet to intensify the effect, increase the pain.

Even when the victims confessed, they still had to be punished for their crimes.

They forfeited all their assets to the Crown and Church, and then were put to death."

When he said "death," we were next to the dead boar. Between the sight of the boar and Juan's explanation, a wave of disgust swept over me. I did what I could to control it, and asked how he had managed to survive.

He poked at the boar and turned a deaf ear.

"You didn't answer my question," I insisted.

He hesitated, took a deep breath, "Being a graduate engineer from the University of Salamanca—the oldest university in Spain, founded in 1218," he paused as if he had said enough.

"Go on."

He sighed. "When I was about to be appointed as the King's Chief Engineer, someone accused me of being a Converso. I had to get beyond the reach of the Inquisition. The safest place was to go to the New World; where skilled and well-educated Jewish men and women were tolerated—as long as they didn't practice Judaism. I bribed a ship's captain set to go to St Augustine to smuggle me on board."

His demeanor suddenly changed. Spreading his arms wide, he proclaimed, "And here I am."

שׁשׁשׁ

Birds screeched, and squirrels scampered from tree to tree; the forest was alive with sound. The carcass's weight nearly pulled my shoulders out of their sockets, as we trudged back to the cabin.

Thoughts of the *strappado* crossed my mind, as we approached a magnificent old oak with a heavy low-hanging branch. Juan threw a thick rope over the branch and with sore arms; we pulled the boar up high off the ground.

שׁשׁשׁ

As we entered the cabin, Carol popped up from her chair, with a book in hand.

Shocked, Juan said, "You can read!"

A smile crossed her face. "I'm reading *All for Love*, by John Dryden."

He laid his hand over his heart. "One never tires of him; he's an author of true, heroic tragedies."

Carol sighed and closed her eyes.

שׁשׁשׁ

After dinner, Juan stated, "To be above suspicion, you will need Spanish identities." He took Carol's hand and spoke, "It will be an honor Carol if you use my mother's name, Señorita Catalina de Aviles."

She cast her eyes down, and replied, "Juan, it's my honor to have your family's name."

"No, I am honored, Señorita Catalina de Aviles." He smiled and turned to me. "And Joel, what name shall we give you?"

"Carlos." The name rolled off my tongue.

"Why that name?"

"He's a famous Spanish author, Carlos Ruiz Zafon."

"I'm not familiar with his works."

Oh! *Of course, the book wouldn't appear until 1993. Oh God, now I've done it. How can I tell him the truth?*

I gulped the wine, gathering my thoughts. "Juan, we are not from Pensacola, we're from a distant land where the government and religion are separate entities."

"What are you talking about, a country without an official religion?"

By this time, Carol had too much wine and became loose-lipped. "The English will send a fleet, so they can control the shipping lanes to Europe."

"What she means is that we traveled through the English colony at Charlestown, and while having lunch in a tavern, overheard officers talking about Governor Moore outfitting twenty or more ships with two months' of supplies, and then promising the men Spanish gold as their reward."

Juan sprung to his feet, his pupils enlarged, "Twenty ships won't be enough to invade Hispaniola, but it's more than sufficient to overtake St. Augustine. We'll have to notify the governor. Both of you must accompany me to verify what you have just said. We will leave in the morning."

Señora Maria De Zuñiga

Juan rowed at a steady pace towards the Castillo. The air is filled with the sounds of the oar's splashing and seagulls' screeching. It was low tide when we approached the dock. At the base of the Castillo's seawall, we could see the guards on the drawbridge, in the sally port.

Juan called out, "We need to see the governor immediately." A voice answered, "It is impossible to see the governor now."

"Why?"

"He's inspecting the western defenses at Fort Peyton; he is expected back soon as Señora Maria de Zuñiga, is incapacitated with one of her severe headaches."

Carol stepped up and asserted. "I can help her. My name is Señorita Catalina de Aviles, and I am an apothecary. Does she suffer them often?"

"Yes. Nothing is effective in healing her pain. She takes to her bed for days, two or three times a month."

I added my two cents' worth, "My sister is a great healer. She can cure her sickness."

"I'm sorry. You still can't see the governor or the Señora without an appointment."

Juan surprised by my response, smiled at the guard. "Sir, after the governor learns you are partly responsible for her cure, he will be so grateful, you'll get a promotion."

With that, the guard stood straighter and thought a moment. Then he pointed, "Walk straight ahead. You will come to a house in the middle of the green.

Tell whoever comes to the door, that I, Lopez," he paused, tapping his chest, "gave you permission to see the Señora to help her with her headache."

We thanked him. However, before Carol left to see the Señora, she instructed Juan and me to gather willow bark, boil it down, and then bring the concentrated liquid to her at the governor's house.

שׁשׁשׁ

A dark-skinned servant was waiting for Juan and me when we returned with a small pot of liquefied willow bark.

He escorted us to a sitting room and bowed slightly. "Please make yourselves comfortable." Juan handed him the pot and off he went.

It was a couple of hours before Carol entered the sitting room where we waited. Juan leaped to his feet, went quickly to her, and put his jacket around her shoul-

The Relic: Jerusalem to St. Augustine

ders, and they both sat down on the couch. I sensed more than mutual concern.

Carol told us what had transpired. "When I got here, a servant was reluctant to let me in.

However, when I said, 'Lopez sent me,' he immediately escorted me to a dark, stuffy room. There, in the bed, propped up on pillows, was the petite, pale Señora Maria de Zuñiga, handkerchief in one hand, a lace fan in the other, which she waved, as if somehow the air would relieve her. Barely audible, she asked, 'Who are you?' I curtsied. 'I am, Señorita Catalina de Aviles, an apothecary.'"

"'But you are a woman!'"

"Ignoring her comment, I went on, 'I will soon have medicine that will make you-better.'"

"Tears slid down her cheeks. She patted them dry, put the fan down, then reached out, took my hand, and cried, 'I can't stand this another minute; my life is not worth living.'"

"I tried to comfort her but felt helpless while waiting for the willow bark.

After a time, a servant brought in the medicine. I thanked him and then instructed him to bring a pot of hot green tea.

He returned shortly with the tea, I poured the willow bark liquid and tea into a cup and held it to her lips. It might have been no more than a few minutes after drinking the tea, her cheeks gradually regained color, and the lines in her brow softened. She smiled, and taking my hand said, 'You are my angel.' "

Juan put his arm around my sister. "My poor Catalina, you have been through so much."

"Juan, my sister is a strong woman." Before I could say another word, a servant came in and announced Señora de Zuñiga would like to see all of us in her room.

There she lay in the large bed encircled by fluffy pillows, clear-eyed and smiling.

"You are as beautiful as always Señora," Juan said.

"You flatter me, Juan," she tilted her head and continued. "Thank you for sending this angel from God. My pain is gone. She has worked a miracle."

I was bursting with pride.

Juan walked over and, tenderly taking the Señora's hand, kissed it.

She blushed. He stepped away and introduced me, then said, "We came to see the governor. We have urgent news."

"My dear friends, your news will have to wait. My husband will not be back until late tomorrow afternoon.

Nevertheless, please, the three of you will be my guest at the Governor's dinner tomorrow night. Señorita Catalina, you shall stay the night with me."

Before Catalina or I could speak, again Juan put his arm around my sister's shoulders and replied, "Señora Maria that will be fine."

Carol now spoke up. "Please now, the two of you, go. The Señora and I must rest."

We bid them goodbye and left.

While Juan rowed the boat back to his cabin, he pressed me to tell him how the concoction of willow bark and tea had cured her. I explained it was a form of aspirin derived from the boiling of willow bark.

"Aspirin? What's that?"

"*Umm...* I'm tired, my dear friend. There are many secrets I have to tell you, but not now."

The Saint from Pensacola

The next day Juan and I stood on the Castillo's gun deck. His eyes shone with pride as he described the fort's construction.

"Carlos, this Fort is made of a local stone called coquina."

I was dying to tell him I knew that and a lot more. He went on, "It consists of tiny shells and fragments held together by sand and lime. There's a coquina quarry near where I live." He paused and said,

"Previous Forts were stockade Forts made from local trees.

I smiled and listened patiently.

"About thirty years ago, a violent storm hit St. Augustine. The waves washed out the stockade's base, causing the walls to collapse under the weight of the guns. It was catastrophic."

He pointed to each of the four corners that jutted out, "Observe how the corners are shaped like arrowheads…" *I wanted to get out of the blistering sun.*

"The cutouts in the angular four corner sides provide cannon crossfire against incoming forces. Observe the narrow walkway connecting the four defensive positions."

He demonstrated with his arms. "There should be cannons all around the entire perimeter walls!" He went silent, a vein in his temple pulsed. "Can you believe they ignored my request, saying it would cost too much and take too long to build?"

I laughed to myself. *Things haven't changed when it comes to government and money.*

"We should return to my cabin and clean up You'll need something appropriate to wear to the governor's dinner."

שׁשׁשׁ

Juan led me to a small room in his cabin where he laid out an outfit for me to wear. I picked up a frilly linen shirt and said, "My sister would love to wear this."

Juan responded, "No, no, this is for a man."

"I'm only kidding. It's very nice, and I'll be proud to wear it."

"I'll return shortly." He smiled and left.

Nevertheless, I still thought, *how my sister would love it.*

He returned a few moments later with a wig and a three-cornered hat. "You will make a fine-looking gentleman when you wear these," he said.

After dressing, we started back to the fortress.

שׁשׁשׁ

It was dusk when we arrived at the governor's house. A guard let us in; we followed a servant through a long, music-filled hall.

Magnificent paintings of Saints Matthew, Mark, Luke, and John, looked down at us he led us to an open double doorway and announced us.

We mingled among the guests, my heart filled with pride, hearing conversations about how the stranger from Pensacola cured the governor's wife.

There was a drum roll, and everyone quieted and turned to the entrance where a broad-shouldered servant stood aside at the open door. He then proceeded to present Governor de Zuñiga, Señora Maria de Zuñiga, and Señorita Catalina de Aviles.

Juan whispered, "Your sister looks stunning."

I nodded, "Yes, radiant."

A frilly lace cap, with streamers, caressed her shoulder-length blond, cascading ringlets, accentuating the dress' square neckline. A tight pearl necklace encircled her throat.

It wasn't long before a servant announced that dinner was being served. We filed into an adjoining dining room. I sat on the governor's left, Catalina next to the governor's wife. Juan occupied a seat next to my sister, displacing the assigned guest to a seat farther down the table. I was concerned this might cause a problem, but nobody seemed to care.

One of the guests was heard to say, of Catalina, "She is the Saint from Pensacola.

The governor loudly acclaimed, "Yes, it is true; Señorita Catalina de Aviles cured my wife. What can be more important than that?!"

Between the entrée and dessert courses, Juan stood and all conversations ceased as Juan raised his voice.

"Ladies and Gentlemen, my new friends, Senor Carlos de Aviles, and his sister Señorita Catalina de Aviles have traveled through Charlestown and have important news for us."

I rose from my chair, "The English at Charlestown are preparing twenty ships with many men, and are promised Spanish gold."

The snickering from many guests greeted my announcement. The governor arched a bushy brow, and laughed, "Our spies tell us they are raising an expedition to find the fabled isle of Bimini with its gold mines, which we know does not exist. So relax, fill your cup, and enjoy."

Shrugging my shoulders, I slumped back into my chair. *I was not taken seriously.*

As the evening drew to a close, the governor's wife made it clear that she wished my sister to stay with her again for the night. A servant provided Juan and me with a lantern to light our way to the boat. Once outside, I took off my hat and wig.

Juan commented, "More comfortable, my friend?

"Yes."

"I'm sorry; nobody took your news seriously. What must we do to protect St Augustine?"

How was I going to tell him the truth about Carol and myself, and convince him to believe what the future held?

When I didn't answer right away, Juan changed the subject. "Look, my friend, how the water reflects the moon and stars."

"Juan you must hear me out," I protested.

"My friend, you're upset."

I closed my eyes and prayed; *please give me the right words to say.*

"My sister and I are not from any country that you've heard of.

There are reasons why you are not familiar with the willow-bark cure and why you're not familiar with the famous Spanish author Carlos Ruiz Zafon."

He stopped rowing, dumbfounded he said, "What? Then where the blazes are you from?"

"We are from the twenty-first century."

Juan shook his head in disbelief.

"It's true. My sister knows all about medicines that will be discovered hundreds of years from now, and I know what the future holds for you, and what will happen soon!"

"And what is that?"

"Colonel James Moore will invade St. Augustine, the city will burn, but the Castillo will hold. Moreover, the treasury building will be looted. If we act quickly, we can change history!"

"You're crazy," then Juan laughed, "too much sangria for you?"

I wanted to scream. "No, it's true. I'm not lying to you, my friend!"

He rubbed his chin. I could see him trying to digest what I'd just told him. If the roles were reversed, would I believe me? Probably not.

Juan nodded his head slowly. "It is hard to believe! But I do trust you and Catalina. St. Augustine and the treasury must be saved at all cost."

Relieved that Juan agreed, we continued around Bird Island without another word, lost in our own thoughts. When we entered his cabin, Juan gave me pause when he asked, "Just how do you suggest we secure the gold, and keep St Augustine from burning?"

"I have an idea, my friend. I've given it great thought…."

Invasion

The sounds of thunder, at sunrise, awoke me from a deep sleep.

Juan prodded me, "Did you hear that?"

"Of course, How could I not? It's thunder."

"That's not thunder, it's cannon fire!"

I swung my feet to the floor and glanced in the direction of the noise. "What are you talking about?"

"It is cannon fire, and it's coming from the sea. We are under attack! Hurry and get dressed," he commanded.

The Relic: Jerusalem to St. Augustine

As he turned to leave, I grabbed his arm. "What is today's date?" The tenth of November, why do you ask?"

"I thought it was the ninth.

This attack will last fifty-one days—the city will be destroyed, the treasury looted! We must go to the mainland now!"

"I don't know, Carlos."

"Don't know what? Just get us out of here now."

"My boat won't do us any good since it's in sight of the English."

I agonized about how my mistake of one day had changed everything. Another loud boom echoed through the cabin, and we both jumped.

Dear God, I thought, *what's going to happen to Carol?*

"If we stay here we will be caught and imprisoned." Another boom, this time closer. Juan continued, "There is an old canoe not far from here. We could take it. It's only a short paddle to town."

שׁשׁשׁ

Briars tore at our clothes; bugs attacked us as we made our way to the waters' edge facing St Augustine. There the canoe lay with a gaping hole in its side.

Juan wiped the sweat from his brow and told me to do as he did. He took off his shirt; I did the same. We stuffed the hole with our shirts.

I held one hand over the shirts to keep it sealed while paddling with my other. Juan was behind me, paddling like crazy with both hands.

We were about a hundred feet from the island when the canoe started to take on water. I was mistaken to think that was the worst of it. There was more to come.

Juan yelled, "There's an English patrol boat! Get down, get down!"

Musket balls whizzed over our heads.

"Do what I do," Juan ordered.

I followed his every move; jumping into the water, grabbing and rolling the canoe over us. We took turns gulping for air at the hole.

The Relic: Jerusalem to St. Augustine

We clung tightly as we frantically kicked our way to the island. Getting out from under the canoe, we ran and ducked behind a sand dune.

The sound of the muskets' fire got closer—the Castillo's cannon fire exploded, followed by the echo of a cannonball landing nearby in the water.

English sailors' voices' carried across the water. "Mates, let's get out of here!"

I thought they were gone and stood up only to see an English patrol boat directly in the Castillo's line of fire.

Another cannonball landed only yards from its port side, creating a geyser that rose a good twenty feet into the air, soaking the patrol boat's crew. They rowed away in panic.

"Juan, how are we are going to get over to St. Augustine without the canoe?"

"Swim, of course!"

A good thing I was on my college swim team.

After the arduous swim, we slithered up the dune to make sure that we were clear of English patrols.

Red and orange fingers of flames shot up from St Augustine. The air was thick with billowing gray smoke, and glowing embers that floated in the air.

I prayed that we would find the treasure–and Carol–quickly and intact.

Juan whispered, "Did you hear that?"

"Hear what?" *How can he hear anything but the crackling of fire and the collapsing of buildings?*

"It's a donkey braying."

"You have very keen hearing, Juan." We set out in that direction.

Not far away, attached to a cart, was a donkey covered in ashes with his ears pushed back, eyes fixated, blocked in by rubble. The poor thing couldn't move. A coquina wall collapsed onto his cart; the axle and wheels were broken into pieces. We did our best to free him but to no avail. We had no other choice but to let him fend for himself.

We resumed our task. Gray smoke choked us. We heard coughing in the distance. Juan called out, "Who's there?"

A hoarse voice responded, "Hola, hola."

"Do you need help? Are you all right?" Juan yelled.

Emerging from the smoke, a hunched over woman carrying a beat-up basket came closer. She put her basket down, and with the sleeve of her dress wiped her face clean.

It was my sister! She ran to us, embraced me and with a muffled voice she said, "I was worried that the two of you would be captured on the island."

As she turned to Juan, he took her arm and asked, "What are you doing here, Catalina? It's too dangerous to be outside the fort."

Tears streamed down her face.

She explained, "One of the governor's daughters took ill late yesterday. He requested I attend to her, knowing that the attack would be today."

Pointing to her basket, she went on. "There are medical supplies in there. I stayed the night. Just before daybreak, I went down to the dock and saw the English were massing for an attack. I ran back to the Fort, screaming, 'The English are attacking, everyone to the Castillo.' Within minutes, bells rang; people were hysterical running up and down the streets."

I thought, *my little sister, a real-life hero. She saved hundreds of lives.* I smiled at her. "If we were home, you would receive the Congressional Medal of Honor. I am so proud of you."

"Congressional Medal of Honor, what is that?" Juan asked.

We ignored his question.

"Dearest sister, how do all the people fit into the fort, with all their dogs, horses, donkeys, cows, and chickens?"

"They don't. Only the people and their cats were allowed into the Castillo; the rest of the animals are kept in the dry moat." Catalina's voice rose. "Do you know what that stupid governor did?

I did know but said nothing.

"He set fire to the homes surrounding the fort, thinking it would keep the English at a distance."

Juan

Small fires glowed, smoke drifted from burnt-out structures. I should have been more concerned with the dire situation, but all I could think of was we were going to be rich.

Our pace picked up as we approach the Treasury building. We made our way through the rubble to the front door. As Carol reached to grasp the latch, Juan cut her off and warned, "Don't open that door. The English may be in there."

She quickly took her hand away. "Oh!"

Juan took charge. "Catalina, you are to stay here. We'll come back for you." He kissed her cheek and then waved to me.

"Carlos, follow me."

I worried about leaving my sister behind but knew I couldn't stand there and do nothing.

Juan and I made our way along the charred walls. "Listen for any unusual sounds, my friend; and when you come to a slit, any opening in the wall, crouch under it."

"Slit?"

"Yes, slits in the wall allow a defender's musket to protect the Treasury building."

Before we turned the corner, Juan stole a searching look down the side of the building, "I don't see any muskets."

Hugging the coquina wall, we made our way methodically to the rear of the building.

When we turned the last corner, I saw that the building's rear wall had collapsed.

"This is a sign from God. It will be safe for us to enter," I muttered.

ששש

Juan led the way in the arduous task of crawling up and over the rubble. The silence was tomb-like. A nauseating stench made it hard to breathe.

The debris crumbled beneath us. Vestiges of now-fragmented coquina cut into my skin.

"Juan, we must get back to my sister now."

"Of course."

I tripped over a dead Spanish guard. My stomach turned.

Juan said, "Catalina should not see such a sight."

"Juan, she's used to seeing dead bodies."

He gave me a surprised silent look, and then said, "But she is a woman!"

"She was going to be a doctor."

Shaking his head, he said, "I've never heard of such a thing—a woman doctor?"

I let it go.

When we reached the door where Carol was waiting, it was blocked by ruins. I could hear her calling, "Is it safe to come in?" She rattled the door as we cleared the way.

"It's okay. Now try it," I called back to her.

Juan chided, "Not so loud."

When the door opened, we were united, she asked, "Did you find the treasure?"

Juan responded, "It's not in this area, we will have to search further."

With that, we stumbled through the rubble to a partially open interior door.

The room was small and musty. Two large wooden chests sat on the floor, side by side. I stared at the chests for a moment; *Papa was right!* Catalina and I smiled at each other, knowingly.

The chests were unlocked. Juan opened one, leaned over and scooped up a handful of gold coins, letting them cascade through his fingers.

My sister's eyes were wide and glowing.

Lying on top of the mountain of gold was a breastplate, adorned with twelve gemstones in four rows of three. *Papa was right again! This must be Aaron's Breastplate!*

Juan broke into my thoughts. "We will have to hide these chests."

"Of course."

Catalina asked, "How? Where? There's no way..." At that moment, I heard something.

"Shush, listen.

Do you hear that?" Juan put his arm around her waist. "Take heed, my dear Catalina. It sounds like it is coming from the back of the building.

A moment later, she nodded. "Yes, I hear it!"

"Catalina, not so loud! We don't know what's out there."

שׁשׁשׁ

I was scared. If it turned out to be a trap and we become prisoners, then what?

To my great relief, it was only the donkey; we thought we had left behind. There he stood, with drooping head, remnants of the cart still attached to his harness.

My sister patted him, and said, "You'll be okay."

Juan said, "Carlos we can make an Indian-drag out of that cart. We will be able to transport the chests to my cabin."

"And just how will we do that?" I asked.

"It's simple; we'll remove what's left of the cart's sides and rear, leaving only the floor.

Without a rear axle, the back of the floorboard will touch the ground at about a forty-five-degree angle. We'll use these three round beams to make rollers."

Though we were exhausted, motivation drove us to accomplish the task.

Accompanied by a cacophony of grunting, we slid each chest, in turn, onto the two rollers. We then placed the third roller in front and finally rolled each chest in turn onto the donkey's drag.

"OK, let's go."

Snakebite

Juan led the donkey by the bridle. He halted abruptly and pointed to a burnt-out blacksmith shop. "We must stop here and take some supplies."

He commandeered a short ax and other tools, while we searched for food.

By the time we left the city and neared the Matanzas River, the wind had picked up. The sun had a halo around it, a sign of an impending storm.

Juan pointed in the direction of some fallen pine trees. "That is how we will get across, my friends. We'll do the same as when the Castillo was being built.

They ferried coquina stone blocks across the river on rafts made from logs and planks."

"And just what are we going to use for paddles?" my sister wanted to know.

"We simply use the thick long tree branches as push poles, to reach the other shore."

It sounded easy until we had to push the chests onto the raft. That was a Herculean task. After Juan and I completed the unloading, we went back for Catalina and the donkey.

Straight-faced, I warned, "Watch out for the alligators ...."

A gust of wind dragged her voice ... "Al-li–gators? I'm not going!"

Juan looked me in the eye, and shouted, "Carlos, you should not tease your sister!" He looked adoringly into her eyes, and said, "He's playing with your feelings. I would not let anything bad happen to you."

I bristled. "Neither would I."

Juan's laugh was tired but genuine. "Carlos, now let us get to work."

I grabbed the bridle and attempted to pull the donkey onto the makeshift raft, but the terrified animal stubbornly refused to budge.

"Having a bit of a problem, my friend?"

I didn't like Juan's sarcasm.

My sister came over. "Watch," she lightly stroked the donkey behind his ear and whispered, "Please go on the raft."

Juan stood next to my sister, laughing, "You two don't know anything about donkeys. This is what we will do. Catalina, you pull on the bridle while we push on the rump."

I was less than thrilled to be behind the donkey. The donkey brayed and I prayed—*don't kick me.*

Juan counted, "One, two, three—push." The donkey moved. Strong wind gusts blew the sand. We choked and coughed as we reassembled the cart.

שׁשׁשׁ

The Relic: Jerusalem to St. Augustine

Upon entering the forest hammock, the wind calmed down, replaced by suffocating heat.

Juan guided the donkey while holding my sister's hand as we trekked.

I was exhausted and ready to pass out when Juan said, "We'll stop here." He tied the donkey to one of the pine trees."

Thank God.

After securing the animal, Juan turned to see my sister reaching for a shrub's fan-shaped branch.

He yelled, "Don't touch that!"

She jumped back. "Why not?"

He walked over to her and held her hand, "My dear, at the end of that lovely fan are sharp, saw-like teeth." He smiled.

After eating and making plans for the next day, we rubbed wax myrtle insect repellant all over ourselves. Looking like purple people, we laughed at each other and then went to sleep.

A rain drizzle awakened me at dawn. The donkey was swinging his tail in all directions to swat away the mosquitos' swarms.

My sister was asleep, nestled against Juan's shoulder. I shook him awake.

After eating some berries and leftovers from the night before, we spread more wax myrtle on our bodies and then hooked up the donkey.

When we neared his cabin, Juan said, "We'll need shovels. Stay here. I'll get them from the shed."

Juan returned, threw the shovels and ropes onto the drag, then pointed to the hillcrest behind his cabin,

"We will bury the chests up there. Then we won't have to worry about the water table."

At the crest, a grove of oaks surrounded a clearing. "This is where we'll dig," Juan said.

Catalina started to pick up a shovel. Juan went to her and took it from her. "No, you should not do this!

"Juan, I must help."

"Shoveling is not women's' work. Carlos and I will do all that is needed."

It was an arduous task. My muscles quivered, but if Juan could keep digging, so would I.

Juan finally gave a loud shout. "Enough!" He hoisted himself up out of the hole. He extended his hand toward me and out I went, too.

We placed the ropes around the chests and then lowered each in turn into its grave. To mark the place, Catalina carved her initials into a nearby tree.

After filling the hole and spreading leaves and twigs over the area as camouflage, Juan said he was going to find a suitable marking stone.

The next thing I heard was Juan's voice, which was unnerving. 'Help Snakebite! Help! Snakebite!"

We rushed over to him. He stood next to an oak tree holding his arm, shrieking, "Pygmy rattlesnake."

My sister told him, "Sit down. You'll be alright."

Two puncture wounds stood out in an area of swelling and redness just above his wrist.

Tears ran down my sister's face. "Joel...I mean Carlos, he needs antivenin and a syringe." The PRM Pharmaceutical Supply in St. Augustine will have what we need." Her eyes pleaded with me to understand. "They know me there."

"No, you can't go back. Only the first son of a pure bloodline can speak God's name and live."

"That's a superstition," she countered, "I'm a Kohen and just as pure as you.

Think logically. In God's eyes, all humankind is equal. God does not have a gender preference." I knew she was right. I didn't want her to be, but I knew she was.

Juan groaned, and in a voice, that was barely audible, asked, "Back to where?"

Her fingers trembled as she placed them on his lips, "Hush— rest—we'll tell you later."

We carefully placed Juan on the drag and took him to his cabin. With Juan resting in his bed, I was still faced with the fear of my sister calling out God's name even though I understood her logic.

"Just do as I did at the Fort, call out God's holy name, and say the special prayer we memorized, and you'll be transmuted to 2012."

I gave her a hug and a kiss on the cheek, and without saying another word, she left to fulfill her quest.

שׁשׁשׁ

It seemed like only a few minutes later when my sister came bursting through the cabin door with the antivenin in hand.

We hugged, and she asked, "Is he alright?"

"He's in his room. He was still with us when I last checked."

I watched from the doorway as she took out a syringe, and a vial, and gave him the shot.

She held his hand and spoke softly. "Sleep, the medicine will take effect, and you'll feel better."

It didn't take long before he fell back asleep.

Catalina spoke with mixed emotions, "When I got back, I went to Papa's home to change my dress. Remember the five swords wall display?"

"Yes."

"It always reminded me of the rays of a rising sun. The one in the center has the initials JC on the blade. Papa said it belonged to our ancestors."

"Yeah," I said, even as I wondered what she was getting at.

"Do you think the JC could be us? Joel and Carol?"

I shook my head. "I don't know."

"Before I left, I called Professor Arenofsky and told him that we had found the breastplate and you will be contacting him soon.

He insisted it was urgent that you meet him immediately upon our return, at Papa's warehouse on Dobbs road. You must go; I'll stay here to take care of Juan. The professor said he wanted to see only you. But be careful of him. Remember what Papa told us."

Juan called out, "Catalina."

We ran to him. He was looking much better. I realized that I was immensely relieved that he would recover. He'd shown himself to be a good friend and without much coaxing. I liked him a great deal, even if his bossiness got under my skin at times.

"What are you two whispering about, out there?" he asked with a tired smile. Carol went and sat beside him on the edge of the bed. She smoothed back his dark hair with her fingers.

"I've got to go back to our time, Juan. I have business there–family business–that I have to see to."

He glanced at Carol and looked as though he could cry. "And you, as well, Catalina?"

Carol looked at me, and I returned her gaze. It would seem my little sister had grown up all over again.

"Not right now, Juan. Catalina will stay with you and make sure you are all better before she comes back home."

She took Juan's hand in hers and with chin held high, she said to me, "While I will miss hot showers and indoor plumbing, I think I'm going to stay here with Juan long after he's healed."

She looked down at her hands and raised them toward me. The gloves were gone, and I had no idea when that had happened. But more amazingly, she had all of her fingers in perfect working order.

She nodded. "Somehow, I'm whole here, my brother. With my pharmaceutical knowledge, I will be of value as an accepted member of the community."

I felt tears filling my eyes, and I looked away. For many years, I loathed our intertwined relationship, and now I knew I'd miss Carol beyond comprehension. Were our destinies to be so different, when? Father is in one time, Carol in another, and me, still another? I shook my head.

The Relic: Jerusalem to St. Augustine

"I don't like it. You don't belong here. We're of a different time."

She laughed. "What is time to us Kohen's anyway? Just think of the interesting reunions we will have."

I laughed, though I still hated leaving her behind. And yet, did we ever leave those we love behind?

"Carlos," Juan said, "You can count on me, I'll protect her. Please do not worry. She is the light of my days since I first met her."

She beamed. "See, dear brother? I'll be fine. You go back to St. Augustine and take care of whatever the Professor wants."

"You've changed in the time we've been on this journey. I'm proud of you, and I know how strong you are, but I've looked out for you a long time. Are you sure you want to do this?"

"You've looked out for me too long, but I appreciate it all. I'll be safe and happy," she said, giving Juan a look that told me she was rapidly falling in love. Another first in our lives.

I took a deep breath. "I understand. Let's give this arrangement a short trial. I'll come back in a few months and see if you still feel the same."

"Okay. Now, you go and take care of everything. But promise me you won't just pop in and out on me. Let me have some time to find my way, okay?"

Juan interjected, "Do not worry. I'll take excellent care of her."

I kissed her cheek and shook Juan's good hand. "Don't go getting married without me. Give me a date, and I'll be here."

Part III

Seek the LORD while he may be found; call on

him while he is near.

Isaiah 55:6-7

Revelation

Faster than a hummingbird takes nectar from a flower, I went directly to Papa's house, called the professor and arranged to meet him at the Dobbs Road warehouse. I had time to shower, take a nap and put on clean clothes.

It looked as though the place was ready to collapse. Leaves and debris crunched underfoot as I walked unsteadily on the broken path that leads to green-mold-covered cement steps.

The worn doorknob squeaked, the rusty hinges squealed as I opened the door and stepped inside. Light from dirt-smeared windows afforded little illumination.

All I could think about was Carol, and how much I'd miss her.

"Is anyone here?" I called. My voice echoed.

A deep voice resonated from above, "Da professor is wait'in up here for ya."

Two tough looking men stood on a narrow, elevated metal walkway. One of them pointed to a metal staircase and motioned that I should use it.

"Up here. He's wait'in for ya. In de shipping office."

I knew there was a problem, but didn't see any alternative than to climb those stairs where trouble waited for me. God had stayed with us this far, I had to believe He still had me in his sights. At least Carol was safe, and Papa was happy.

They stood behind me. One of them said, "Walk."

I couldn't imagine why the professor would have these hoodlums working for him.

We walked a little way, then suddenly there was a sharp pain in the back of my head, and everything went black.

שׁשׁשׁ

"Joel, Joel, wake up." Someone shook my shoulders.

A naked light bulb swung from a long chord. Stale cigarette smoke choked me. My head throbbed.

My wrists were duct-taped to the chair. I protested. "What the hell's going on?"

"There's no time left!" said Professor Arenofsky. The thugs were standing next to him. "I've been watching your father's house. You've gone back and found the treasure. Where is it?"

I gently shook my head to try to clear my thoughts, but the headache wasn't helping. "I don't have it."

He scowled, took a step closer. "I must have Aaron's breastplate! Where is it?"

The Relic: Jerusalem to St. Augustine

Struggling to get my hands free I shouted, "Let me go! My head hurts, and I told you, I don't have it!"

"Your sister left a message that you've found Aaron's breastplate. I must have it now!"

I struggled to understand. *Please God, help me.* None of this made sense. Professor Arenofsky was Papa's life-long friend. "We found it, but I couldn't bring it back," I said. One of the men eyed me with a stare that could remove acid from a car battery.

The professor's face darkened, he shifted his weight and started again. "My buyer will be here soon to pick up the breastplate. I will stop at nothing to get it!"

"I can't give you what I don't have."

"Do you know what the source of the worst pain is Joel?" It's the nerves in your teeth; that's because they're so close to your brain."

I swallowed hard, determined not to faint.

"These boys will break each tooth in sequence, exposing the nerve in each, until you talk."

This can't be happening! Mortified, I heard myself respond, "I told you we don't have it."

The professor came close and held up a red string between his fingers, "Your Rachel String can't help you now!" Then he stepped back, turned and said, "Keno, proceed."

Keno crushed out his cigarette on the table—lumbered around to the back of my chair—grabbed a handful of my hair—pulled back until my mouth opened. I stiffened in anticipation of the pain. The other man returned with pliers from the table, waving them a few inches from my face.

He laughed. "I'm gonna enjoy hearing you scream."

I strained at my bindings as Keno pulled my hair back harder. The cold metal pliers touched my lips, and I scrunched my eyes closed. I wanted to die!

At that moment, a distinctive sound of a gunshot rang out followed by a dull thud.

My hair released, I opened my eyes. Standing before me were two men in dark business suits armed with Uzis.

Keno lay on the floor in a pool of blood. Standing next to the body was a woman, with red hair tied in a bun, holding a smoking 45. My God, it was Ms. Krief.

"Cut his bonds," she ordered.

ששש

I was bewildered, yet relieved. When I saw a red-knotted string on her wrist, I knew my ordeal was over. "Ms. Krief..."

She stepped on my words. "No. I am Captain Freeman of the Mossad, the Israel secret service. Your father worked for us from time to time. He told us about the breastplate, but he died before revealing its location. We had no reason to suspect Professor Arenofsky.

He planned to use Aaron's breastplate as an excuse for an Egyptian general to start a war with Israel. But the general died this morning, just a few minutes after his plane landed in Miami."

She ordered her men, "Clean up the mess. Make sure the Professor and the remaining thug disappear."

"Was that you in the plaza?"

"Yes. We had you and your sister under constant surveillance, from that moment near the Casa Monica when a gunshot narrowly missed you; which had nothing to do with the two of you.

"What about that time in the helicopter?" I asked.

We watched you from a helicopter. A shark was closing in on you. So I shot at it."

"Wow!"

"Joel, your father was a hero. We wouldn't have won the Six-Day War without his help."

Handing me her card, she said, "Joel, please consider serving the best interests of America, Israel, and the world by returning the breastplate to Israel. We know that you haven't brought it back with you, but the world, you and your sister will be safer when it is returned to us. And, of course, you can keep the gold."

Dumbstruck and humbled by her offer, I thanked her and put her card in my wallet. "It isn't here. It isn't anywhere at this time," I murmured through the pounding in my head.

She stared at me a long moment but didn't say a word. Then she nodded. Still wobbly on my feet, I started to leave when she asked if I needed any help.

"No, I'll be fine," I lied. I just needed to get home where I could think.

1702

Showered, fed and rested at Papa's house, I contemplated what explanation I could offer to those who inquired about Carol's absence. She's on sabbatical; No, a work-study program in Europe...or a cruise around the world.

Who was I kidding? No one would believe me. I'd probably be arrested for killing her and sentenced to life in prison because she's just suddenly vanished. This Kohen thing certainly hadn't made life any easier.

In addition, there was my promise to leave Catalina to her own devices, at least for a while. How would I ever have the restraint to do that?

So many questions—is a month's time the same in time travel as it was at this time?

שׁשׁשׁ

On the refrigerator door is a calendar that Carol placed there, with her notes written all over it. After reflecting on the calendar, I had an epiphany. *The physical location remains constant. However, I can go to any point in time, past or future! Paradoxically, Carol's future is still in the past.*

The Government House was mostly destroyed during the English bombardment of 1702. Therefore, it would be a safe place to reappear on the evening of May 11, 1703.

Later that evening, I went to the small park behind the Government House building and transmuted to 1703.

I was just in time to see the Night Watch assembling for their torch-lit march down St. George Street to the Castillo de San Marcos.

שׁשׁשׁ

Early the next morning, I rented a rowboat. All I could think of was *how happy I'd be when we're all together.*

My heart sank when I saw how drastically things had changed.

The once carefully tended cabin was overgrown with vines and spider webs. In the cabin, I found old books covered in dust and mold. The cabin, in effect, had been abandoned.

I knew Carol and Juan couldn't just disappear without a trace. *I must go to Governor Zuñiga. He will know their whereabouts.*

Weary, I returned to the boat and rowed to the Castillo.

The sentry at the entrance wouldn't let me in. I insisted I had to see the governor. Luckily, Juan's old friend Lopez heard the commotion and joined us. After a few expiations, I was let in.

The Relic: Jerusalem to St. Augustine

A servant at Governor Zuñiga's residence led me down the familiar narrow hall lined with paintings of the Saints.

We stopped at an ornately carved door. He knocked before opening it into a long narrow conference room. High-ranking officials, in ladder-back chairs, sat around a massive wooden conference table.

The governor rose from his chair, and exclaimed, "Carlos, what has happened to you? Where have you been?"

All eyes focused on me.

Shifting from foot to foot, I stated, "Please, I'm trying to find Juan and Catalina. Do you know where they are?"

Tense glances were exchanged among those gathered. No one answered.

Governor Zuñiga broke the uncomfortable silence. "I'm sorry. I can't help. We haven't seen them for quite a while."

Some of the officials nodded in agreement, while others shifted their eyes away.

He came over to me, put his arm on my shoulder, and whispered into my ear,

"If we can be of any further assistance to you—in any way—please don't hesitate to ask." He then shook my hand and said, "Come back anytime."

I knew I was getting the politician's shuffle, but why?

I thanked him, and then asked a favor, "Would you be so kind as to let me stay the night, as it is getting dark?"

"Why of course." I spent a restless night thinking *there might be clues at Juan's cabin that would lead me to their whereabouts.*

שׁשׁשׁ

Determined by my desire to find my sister and Juan, before sun-up I journeyed back to the cabin, and went to the shed, took one of the shovels.

The area was overgrown, and the stone marker was hidden. I knew Carol had carved initials in a tree trunk, near the buried treasure. I looked for it. Sure enough, there it was not far from the stone peeking out from some vines.

The Relic: Jerusalem to St. Augustine

I cleared the vines and dug until I heard a thud. Excited, I threw the shovel to one side and scooped away the dirt with my hands, so I could open the lids.

To my shock and horror, both were empty, except for two red strings lying on my sister's gloves, and a handwritten note:

> Dear Brother,
>
> Juan and I sailed to the Danish island of St. Thomas, where there is a large Jewish community; and were married by their rabbi.
>
> Juan knows everything about us. I truly love him. Juan and I didn't want to start our life together living a lie. Therefore, after we returned to St. Augustine, we told the governor that during the invasion, we removed and hid the gold for

safekeeping. The governor then commissioned us to escort the gold to Cuba.

Having been sworn to secrecy,

I can't tell you when we sailed or even the name of the ship; Juan and I should be back from our mission before your return.

I know you would agree, we did the right thing in order to make things whole by giving back the gold.

Forgive me for taking your fortune away. Do not worry if we are delayed.

Love you, brother,
Carol

P.S. We took Aaron's breastplate with us. Now that we are married, we no longer need Rachel's red strings. We are committed to protecting each other.

Dazed and defeated, I placed the letter, gloves, and strings in my backpack, refilled the hole, and headed back to the Castillo. *She took my fortune! Where were they?*

From the sally port, I could see Governor Zuñiga and his wife leaving the Castillo chapel. I ran to them.

When I reached him, he nodded smiled, "My dear Carlos," "What brings you back to us so soon?"

I said not a word and gave him Carol's letter.

He hesitated "What is this?"

"Read it—please—then we'll talk."

Perplexed, he glanced at the letter and then handed it back to me. His demeanor changed. He turned to his wife. "My dear, please return to the house without me. I must speak to Carlos in private."

She smiled. "I understand—men's business. You go ahead. I shall see you later. Carlos, please join us for dinner, if you are still here."

I nodded stiffly.

The governor's eyebrows furrowed, "Follow me." We walked along the seawall, neither of us uttering a word.

Stopping abruptly and speaking rapidly, the governor explained. "Carlos, fifteen years ago, the pirate Robert Searle killed over sixty men, women, and children burned our settlement, and stole our gold from the treasury building."

I grew impatient. *I know all that. Damn it, where is my sister?*

"If it was not for Juan and Catalina removing the gold, it could have happened again! This is why I entrusted them with a mission. They were to take the chests of gold to Havana."

Hesitating, and then taking a deep breath, he continued. "I was informed that everything was lost when their ship sailed into a storm and broke up in the Dry Tortugas."

Tears ran down his cheek. He continued, "Their bodies were recovered. We buried them on an unnamed island.

As the king's representative, I convey to you the Crown's gratitude for Juan's and your sister's extraordinary service.

Due to the secrecy of their mission, tomorrow evening you will attend a small dinner with a few high-ranking officers, the Priest, and of course my wife. I will present—a ceremonial sword—to you. It is the King's personal gift."

I could barely hold back my tears. *Why did they have to die? Why have I waited so long to come back? I'd missed her by a matter of weeks, it seemed.*

As a guest of the governor and his wife, I attended the official dinner hosted in honor of my sister and her husband. All the time thinking: *had she finally been happy*? Somehow, I thought she probably was.

Upon receiving the sword, I nearly fainted when I saw the initials J C engraved in gold on the blade. *It's the very same sword we saw in Papa's house,* I smiled.

Having no reason to stay in the 18th century, I transmuted the next day back to Papa's house in the 21st century.

Without my fortune in gold, I was going to have to get back to work.

ENLIGHTENMENT

Returning to Papa's house in the year 2012 I opened the curtains and drapes, it lightens the room, but not my mood.

I cleaned and organized every closet and drawer, even the attic. I questioned myself. *How did I allow myself to get sucked into such a mess?* Everyone I cared for was dead. Was it Papa's fault, because of his religious zealousness, or could the fault be mine? *Were they truly dead?*

Papa, murdered by his friend; Carol drowned at sea? Nothing makes sense to me. I wander from room to room and reminisce about my childhood.

My love of sailing, and how someday I'd live on a boat and travel around the world. Well, maybe I could still do that.

Princeton sent me an e-mail. When would I be resuming my duties on the faculty? I replied that my father's affairs were still to be settled and that it would be awhile before I would be ready. I had access to Papa's money, though not the wealth, that Spanish gold would have afforded. Yet somehow, without Carol in my world, that didn't matter much.

The dark feelings and confusion persisted until I received a letter from Papa's lawyer, Mr. Graham. It said Papa's estate had to be probated and he needed to see me in his office, at my earliest convenience. *Maybe a new project would help my melancholy.*

שׁשׁשׁ

The lawyer's office was in an old Victorian-style house that sat next to the Limelight Theatre, on Old Mission Avenue; a quiet, tree-lined street just north of the bustle of the Old City.

The Relic: Jerusalem to St. Augustine

I told the receptionist who I was and that Mr. Graham requested that I see him as soon as possible.

"I'm sorry, but he's in court now. He should be back this afternoon. I can pencil you in for 2:45."

"Sure," I said. She took my cell number, and I left.

Directly across San Marco Ave., at the corner of Old Mission Avenue, is the Mission of Nombre de Dios. I had never been there because Papa took us only to non-Christian sights. With time on my hands, I walked over to take a closer look.

A path took me to a footbridge that arcs over a tidal lake. Stopping for a moment at its crest, a sense of tranquility came over me. *This is the most peaceful place I have ever been.*

Facing east towards the lake stands a 208-foot-high cross and the statue of Fr. Francisco Lopez. I gazed at that sight a long time.

I crossed the footbridge to the opposite side and stopped. A few feet away, a tall, commanding figure, probably a teacher, delivered a lecture to a dozen younger men gathered around him. "First Catholic mission in North America," I listened to the history.

He smiles, then motioned for me to come closer.

I returned his smile and walked over.

He introduces himself. "I'm Yeshua Ben Yosef, and these are my students. To my left are Peter and his brother Andy. Next to them are James and his older brother John." Pointing to his right, he continued, "Phil and Bart. Behind them are Matt and another James."
They all laughed.

"And next to them are Tad, Jud, Syd, and Tom. We were just leaving to visit the Chapel of Our Lady of La Leche. You're welcome to join us."

I accepted. We walked along the narrow path and stopped in front of the Rustic Altar. Yehuda explained, "The alter commemorates the first Catholic Mass held here, on September 8, 1565. That's over two-hundred years before the American Declaration of Independence."

We lingered, and then went on to the Chapel of Our Lady of La Leche, which Yehuda told us, "dates back to 1613."

They filed in, but I hesitated and stayed behind.

Yehuda asked me, "Why do you not enter?"

"I'm of the Jewish faith."

He put his hand on my shoulder and quietly stated, "So am I. Remember, my son, every house of God is for all."

Before I could respond, he led me into the chapel.

The room was small. A bank of flickering candles created a warm glow.

He pointed to one of the narrow backless wooden benches, and whispered, "If you like, sit over there."

The students smiled at me, then at each other. The chapel's quietness was unnerving.

A pedestal, in the far right corner, supported a hand-carved and hand-painted statue of Mary, breastfeeding the baby Jesus. *What would Papa think?*

Suddenly there was a startling, brilliant flash of lightning. Moments later came a defining clap of thunder. *Just one of those Florida thunderstorms; it should pass in a few moments.* Then another thunderous burst. I envisioned *Moses at the burning bush and heard God saying, "I am what I will be."*

Another blinding flash and the sound of thunder resonated in my head.

Then before me–*King David on his knees in the Holy of Holies, pleading for God's forgiveness for his mortal sins.*

Sobbing, I bowed my head, ashamed and silently pleaded. *The list of my sins is long. They weigh on me like Marley's chain. God, I am to blame for my sister's death, guilty of the sins of greed, egotism, and arrogance!*

God, I pray for forgiveness and your wisdom. Punish me; make me expiate my faults. I'm ready to accept your judgment and will sacrifice and do anything to set things right and make them whole again.

I felt the room shake. When I opened my eyes, I was alone. Where did they all go?

I decided to leave, in spite of the weather. My senses betrayed what I saw: not a trace of a violent storm. The sky was crystal blue, what was going on? I checked my cell phone.

I'd left the lawyer's office only eighteen minutes earlier, and there was a text from his office. He'd returned earlier than expected, and could see me now.

I looked about again. No sign of the men I entered the chapel with.

It took only a few minutes to arrive at Graham's office.

Mr. Graham was a big man with an even bigger ego. He regarded himself a local celebrity because he was a former States Attorney.

His office was jammed full of Jacksonville Jaguar and University of Florida's football memorabilia. He was obviously well connected, and Papa trusted him.

I executed a power of attorney for him to handle the estate without my participation; because I knew what I had to do.

The one thing Hebrew school taught me is that an apology for a wrong is not sufficient; one is obligated to reverse the wrong. Then and only then, God will forgive the wrongdoer.

Therefore, to be forgiven, I must go back in time to 1986 to re-direct destiny. I could call my mother, change my behavior, and have Carol completely miss that terrible, life-altering incident when she was a little girl.

However, if I did that, would she also miss the love of a man like Juan?

She was truly happy and fulfilled there. In that time, in that place, she was valued beyond measure. She had no deformity. She was respected and revered. It was all authentic. She was gone too soon for my liking, but that time with Juan had defined her life one well lived and given to others. Did I have the right to undo that?

The Relic: Jerusalem to St. Augustine

I recalled Papa quoting Isaiah, Chapter 43:18, *Remember ye, not the former things, neither consider things of old.*

As I walk the streets of St. Augustine on sunny days and sit by the coquina walls of the Castillo, sometimes I even smell the black powder of the cannons. As a Kohen, I am ready to do what must be done.

שׁשׁשׁ

I called my old home number from a pay phone, praying, *Please, God, don't let my mother recognize my adult voice.*

"Hello," Mama said.

Disguising my voice, I said, "Hello is this Mrs. Schwartz?"

"Yes, can I help you?"

"This is Coach Ramsey."

"How can I help you?"

"Just tell Joel the baseball team's practice has been moved back an hour."

"I'll make sure he gets the message. Thank you, good-bye."

I wanted to tell her what had happened, but all I could manage was "Good-bye."

I closed my eyes for a few moments. When I opened them, I was ten years old, standing in my bedroom.

Mama was yelling up to me. "Joel, honey, your coach just called. Your baseball game's practice has been moved back an hour. Get dressed now so you can walk your sister to the birthday party. By the way, I put your glove on your closet shelf."

"Okay, Mama."

On our way to the party, Carol and I approached the overgrown wooded lot.

Carol looked at me and asked, "Do you know what's in there?"

"The Boogie Man!"—we ran past the lot.

GLOSSARY

apothecary: Pharmacist.

barshert: Jewish word for fate.

cravat: cloth often made of and trimmed with lace, worn about the neck by men especially in the 17th century.

chuffed: Make noisy explanations or grunts.

con Leche and a Tarta: Is an open top fruit tart.

Converso: Jews of Spain were a force to profess Christianity, but remain Jews secretly.

Davidic: The line of King David's descendants.

Defense wall of the city: in the twenty-first century is St. George Street.

Drag: Another term for a Travois the Plains Indians of North America, to drag loads over land.

A primitive vehicle common among the North American Indians, usually two trailing poles serving as shafts and bearing a platform or net for a load.

Enthused: meaning inspired, stimulated.

Exodus, 23: Ex. xxviii. 15-21. Thou shalt make the breast-plate of judgment with cunning work, of ruby, topaz, emerald, sapphire, and diamond set in gold

galumph: tromp heavily in a clumsy gait.

Ginevra de' Benci: An aristocratic noblewoman from fifteenth-century Florence.

gunnels or gunwale: The upper edge or planking of the side of a boat.

hardpan: Any layer of firm detrital matter, as of clay, underlying soil.

Hashem: Another reference to God.

hammock: Tropical hardwood hammocks are closed canopy forests, dominated by a diverse assemblage of evergreen and semi-deciduous tree and shrub species, most of West Indian origin.

Hassidic: A member of a religious sect founded in Poland in the eighteenth century; Characterized by the emphasis on mysticism, prayer, ritual strictness, zeal, and joy.

hand-hewn cedar beams: Any long piece of building material that has been transformed from round log to square timber using only hand-held tools.
These timbers can then be sawed to different lengths and used as beams, joists, or trusses.

Hilt: The part of the sword that is not the blade. It consists of the cross guard and the grip.

hogtied: The hogtie when used on pigs and cattle has it where three of the four limbs are tied together, as tying all four together is difficult and can result in harm to the animal.

Jesus (Yehuda): The name Jesus corresponds to the Greek spelling Iesous, from which, through the Latin Iesus, comes the English spelling Jesus. The Hebrew spelling Yehua (עושי) appears in some later books of the Hebrew Bible.

John Dryden: was an English poet, literary critic, translator, and playwright who was made Poet Laureate in 1668.

He is seen as dominating the literary life of Restoration England to such a point that the period came to be known in literary circles as the Age of Dryden, (August 1631 – May 12, 1700).

Kabbalah: Jewish mysticism; understanding the mysteries of God and Creation.

Kaddish: Jewish mourners'' prayer.

Kohen: A direct descent from the biblical Aaron.

kvetching: Jewish term for complaining.

Mathew 9:27NIV: 27: As Jesus went on from there, two blind men followed him, calling out, "Have mercy on us, Son of David!"

mazeltov: Jewish word for congratulations.

Mensch: Someone to admire and emulate. One of noble character.

nachas: Pride or gratification, at the achievements of one's children.

painted lady: A circa 1890's home

pulchritudinous: Beautiful

Rachel's Red Strings: Worn on the left wrist is considered by Kabbalah to be the receiving side of the body and soul. By wearing The Red String, we can receive a vital connection to the protective energies surrounding the tomb of Rachel.

Rosh Hashanah: Jewish New Year.

Sally Port: a forts gateway permitting the passage of a large number of troops at a time.

Salvia Leucantha: Mexican Sage is a perennial. Blueish and velvety soft foliage comes out before autumn urges out their elongated clusters of fuzzy lavender blooms.

Shanda: Shame.

shin (ש): The first letter of the word "Shema," which translates to the word "hear." It is also the 21st letter of the Hebrew alphabet.

Shiva: Seven-day mourning period for the departed

shofar: A trumpet made from a ram's horn.

tabby wall: Original tabby concrete walls of slave housing at Kingsley Plantation on Fort George Island, Florida, USA, built in 1814.

Tabby is a type of concrete made by burning oyster shells to create lime, then mixing it with water, sand, ash and broken oyster shells.

tarta: Cake or open top tart.

Ten Sefirot: The ten creative forces that intervene between the infinite, knowledgeable God and our created world.

Torah: A scroll containing the first five books of the Hebrew Scriptures.

tricorne: A 17th-century three-cornered hat with an upturned brim.

tzitzit: Name for specially knotted ritual fringes, or tassels, worn in antiquity by Israelites and today by observant Jews.

Yit-ga-dal ve-yit-ka-dash she-mei ra-ba: The beginning of an ancient Hebrew prayer for the dead, written in Aramaic.

yakama: A common Kippot (skull cap) worn by Jewish men.

Yeshiva: An academy for the advanced study of Jewish texts (primarily the Talmud).

Yeshua Ben Yosef: Meaning salvation also another name for Jesus Christ.

Yom Kippur: Day of Atonement.

Zafon, Carlos Ruiz: Author of six novels, including the bestsellers The Shadow of the Wind, The Angel's Game and The Watcher in the Shadows.

Reading Group Guide

1. What chapters had the most impact on you?

2. Can the past be changed?

3. What significance does the activity at the Mission of Nombre de Dios mean to you?

4. Is time travel possible?

5. What is the underlying message?

6. Can you associate any of the characters with anyone you have known

BIBLIOGRAPHY

Central Conference of American Rabbis. Gates of Prayer. New York, NY: CCAR Press, 1975.

Corlett, William, and John Moore. The Judaic Law. Scarsdale, NY: Bradbury Press, 1979.

Coyle, Pamela. KA-KA-TUV, As It Is Written. New York, NY: CCAR Press, 2000.

The Florida Historical Quarterly, Tampa, FL: January 1995.

The Florida Historical Society, The Florida Historical Quarterly, Tampa, FL: January 1974.

The History of Castillo de San Marcos, Historic Print & Map Co., St. Augustine, FL: 2005.

Little, Mark. St. Augustine Historical Society. Bishop Verot's Probate Records. St. Augustine, FL: 2006: Excerpts from various articles and journals.

Matt, Daniel C. The Essential Kabbalah. Edison, NJ: Castle Books, 1997.

Shengold Books, The Shengold Jewish Encyclopedia. Rockville, MD, 1998.

St. Augustine 450th Commemoration, "First America Lecture Series 2009–2010."

Webster's New Universal Unabridged Dictionary.

Jo M. Weiss Ph.D. and K. Brad Grunert, Ph.D.: "Wisconsin Medical Journal: Post-traumatic Stress Disorder Following Traumatic Injuries in Adults," 2004, Vol. 103, No. 6, pp 69-72.

Inquirer Wire Services, August 30, 1988.

Study Unwanted Sex Common In the late 1700s.

Quail Bell Magazine, August 21, 2011—Odd-Timey Sex.

Yeshuda Ben Yosef, Yeshua.org/historical-facts/yeshuda-ben-yosef.

ABOUT THE AUTHORS

Betsy S. Lee & K. Ross Lee has co-authored *The Relic: Jerusalem to St. Augustine, Fl.* and *Andrew Ranson: St Augustine's Pirate* (received a finalist 2015 standing in the Royal Palm Literary Awards finalist.) Both books are exciting, mysterious, historical fiction of real people and historic events.

Betsy S. Lee has been a featured author at the Amelia Island Book Festival. She participated in the Florida Heritage Book Festival in St. Augustine.

Among her many prestigious professional affiliations, Betsy is most proud to be a member of the Florida Writers Association and is the past recording secretary of the National League of American Pen Women.

Betsy is an award-winning professional photographer and illustrator. She received a tribute from the Florida House of Representatives for her historical photos that are on permanent display in the Capitol Building in Tallahassee, Florida.

Betsy S. Lee works include:

OFF THE TRACK: Royal Palm Literary Award (First Place)

The Relic: Jerusalem to St. Augustine, co-author K. Ross Lee

Andrew Ranson: St Augustine's Pirate co-author, K. Ross Lee

Off The Track Coloring & Activities Book

Historic ST. Augustine Activities Book

I'm Smarter Than That (play form)

Let's Color & Draw

KRoss Lee (Kalmun Ross Lee), over the years, has written educational monologues of historical characters, several one-act plays, and routines for known standup comedians and a magic comedy team.

During the many years of rigorous religious studies, he developed fervor to search for the effects of religion on history. Kalmun and his wife, Betsy, founded two Reform Jewish congregations in New Jersey and Florida. He led the religious services.

Kalmun's credentials include Memberships in (SAJHS) St Augustine Jewish Historical Society and the (HFS) Historical Fiction Society.

He completed his studies of world investments at the New York School of Finance. After retiring as a floor member specialist, of a major stock exchange, he moved to Florida and became a real estate developer and broker.

Upon selling his business, Kalmun became a licensed city tour guide in St. Augustine, Florida, and certificated guide by the U.S. Department of the Interior for the Castillo de San Marcos.

Please visit our website, *www.betsyslee.com*

www.ingramcontent.com/pod-product-compliance
Lightning Source LLC
Chambersburg PA
CBHW060516100426
42743CB00009B/1340